My book of Genesis

Best wishes

Rol | My — 1

My book of
GENESIS

Richard Macphail
with Chris Charlesworth

Foreword by Peter Gabriel

ISBN 978-1-5272-1504-7

www.mybookofgenesis.com

A catalogue record for this book is available from
the British Library.

Cover design and typesetting by S1/design. www.s1design.london
Printed and bound in Great Britain by CPI Group (UK) Ltd

*I dedicate this book to my mother,
Mary Macphail, to my sisters
Moira Firth and Kate Stevens and
to my wife Maggie Cole.*

CONTENTS

Foreword by Peter Gabriel   9

Acknowledgements   13

Chapter 1   In the beginning   15
Chapter 2   Mick Jagger – the devil incarnate   23
Chapter 3   Anonymous at Charterhouse   33
Chapter 4   The wilderness years   41
Chapter 5   Eyeless in Gaza   53
Chapter 6   The cottage   61
Chapter 7   A little bit of Charisma   75
Chapter 8   Mellotronics   91
Chapter 9   The grand tour   105
Chapter 10   The guy in the top hat   121
Chapter 11   Why I left Genesis   129
Chapter 12   Why did Peter leave Genesis?   143
Chapter 13   The kraken wakes   155
Chapter 14   Busted in St Gallen   167
Chapter 15   I didn't choose Brand X   177
Chapter 16   Birds on the wire   193
Chapter 17   A marriage of convenience   201
Chapter 18   The reunion   209

Appendix   An interview with Steve Hackett   221

BY PETER GABRIEL

White sailor's loon pants, red hair in a close cropped mod haircut, a silky voice and mic technique with more than a few Jaggerisms, all served with a confident strut. This was Richard Macphail, the singer of Anon, the hippest band in the school. They could talk the talk about current and future Bluesbreakers line-ups, had actually been to the Marquee Club and on a good day, could sound quite a bit like the Stones. Watching them perform to the school, I had no idea then how our futures would become interlaced.

My connection with all this was music, loud, soulful music. I would play drums as loud as I could whilst dreaming of singing like Otis and Nina and would play with any band that would let me, with as much raw energy as I could muster. For inspiration, we would turn to the greats of blues and soul music and the new young British bands like The Who, The Animals, The Yardbirds, Family and the unquestioned royalty: The Beatles and the Stones. Although extremely enthusiastic, my skill as a drummer did not match my ambition and I gradually switched my focus to songwriting.

The petri dish in which this music evolved was a British public school in which rock music was frowned upon, discouraged and occasionally, at least for Mike Rutherford, banned. Richard Macphail and Rivers Job, his friend and musical mentor, were important figures in the school's music scene but found themselves sent off to other schools and Tony Banks and I fell into the hole they had left. We were invited to join Ant Phillips and Mike Rutherford in putting some songs together on a demo tape, which we dreamed other people might want to record. We included one of our own songs and the core of the future Genesis was loosely assembled. With the original Anon scattered, I took over the role of singer for these demos that could well have fallen to Rich.

Years later, in 1973, when Genesis put out our first live album, it was dedicated 'to Richard Macphail, who has left us'. Many assumed he had at least died and started to ask who this little known sixth member of the band could be.

Outside of the writing, Rich had contributed in almost every other way possible. He was the band's official chameleon, tour manager, cheerleader, driver, agent, roadie, chef, procurer, repairman, general hustler and counsellor, always helping to smooth over all the predictable 'creative differences' between clashing testosterone-packed young egos. The writing and arrangement of the music was always a tense battle of wills.

When we outgrew the beaten up London taxicab I had bought to carry the band's gear, he managed to persuade his dad to let us have a decommissioned bread van at a knockdown price. When we couldn't afford to find a rehearsal place that would allow us to get our album together over a period of months, he again persuaded his long-suffering parents to help and let us use their soon to be marketed cottage near Dorking. When we weren't able to feed ourselves on the money coming in, Rich learned how to bake bread and made big bowls of yoghurt and of muesli, both of which he prepared at night before we went to bed and which were to become the core of our diet in that snowy winter.

Rich would have the energy and stamina to keep real life functioning around us when all of ours was immersed in the music. At our lowest point, in 1970, we were devastated when Ant, then our most prolific writer, left after developing a fear of performing live. Tony wanted to return to Sussex University (he'd been careful to keep his place open) and I was considering taking a place offered to me at the London School of Film Technique, but Rich had the unstoppable enthusiasm and the belief in a brilliant future that helped to keep us all on board and convince us to give it just one more try.

FOREWORD

There were many wonderful and funny moments in the underfunded and chaotic travels of a young band trying to make it, as you will discover when you read this book. He was our unsung hero and when I eventually left Genesis, it was to Rich that I turned once again as my tour manager, for another two years of travelling adventures. I am happy that his story is now being told.

Peter Gabriel
September 2017

MY BOOK OF GENESIS

ACKNOWLEDGEMENTS

Having retired from my work as an energy consultant, I began discussing the possibility of this book project with my good friends Gail and Glen Colson and they suggested that I might consider working with Chris Charlesworth. I knew Chris from his days at the *Melody Maker* in the early 70s but had lost touch with him. Coincidentally, Chris had also just retired from his job as commissioning editor at Omnibus Books. After an initial meeting at his house in the Surrey Hills, we decided to work together. Thus, once a week over the summer of 2016, I went down to Chris's house and we produced what was to become the first draft of *My Book of Genesis*. As the story unfolded, it transpired that Chris and I had, in many ways, lived parallel lives during our time in the rock music business. It was an enjoyable process and Chris's knowledge of the key players of the era proved to be very useful.

As part of the writing process I wanted to obtain the perspectives of all the original members of the band and I am very grateful to Peter Gabriel, Tony Banks, Mike Rutherford, Phil Collins, Steve Hackett and Anthony Phillips for their generosity and time in making important contributions to this book.

Having completed the first draft, I gave the manuscript to my wife, Maggie Cole. I am extremely grateful to Maggie for her observations and insight from which we worked together to produce the second draft.

In March 2017, the baton was passed to Miranda Davies. Miranda is an accomplished writer and editor. We were at school together in the 60s and we have been friends ever since. Working with her editor's mantra 'if in doubt, leave it out', Miranda scoured her way through the book suggesting many changes and deletions - most of which I agreed to.

As there were no lucrative publishing deals on the horizon, I decided that I would self-publish my book. Producing a manuscript was one thing but how on earth would I turn that into an illustrated book? The answer came from my good friend Charmaine Young, who had recently worked on a book of her own with a graphic designer named Gary Deal from S1/design. Gary was a delight to work with and I could not have done this without him.

I am grateful to Miranda Davies for proofreading and to Chris Charlesworth for the back cover copy and for compiling the index.

Unless otherwise stated, I took all the photographs that we've used. However, I am deeply indebted to my dear friend, Tony Levin, for generously allowing me to use several of his excellent photographs, including the one that we used for the front cover. I am grateful to my nephew, Andrew Firth, for working a little bit of magic with Photoshop. In addition, I would like to thank Mino Profumo, Luca Alberici, Elio Ministeri, Salvo Catania and Helmut Janisch, and all the faithful Genesis fans around the world for their encouragement, friendship and help over the years.

I have received a huge amount of support and encouragement from family and friends with the production of this book. To you all I am deeply grateful.

AUTHOR'S NOTE

All but the last two chapters of this book took place before my 30th birthday in 1980. That was all a long time ago. To the best of my ability, I have tried to recall these events as accurately as possible. There may, however, have been the occasional lapse in my memory. Not everything that you read in this book is necessarily true.

Richard Macphail
West London – September 2017

Chapter 1

IN THE BEGINNING

---

*Being the boy, they had great aspirations for me to be
a lawyer or a doctor or even a man of the cloth.*
Some hope.

'Who needs another blooming book about a bunch of public
schoolboy prog rockers from the 1960s?' I hear you cry.
Undoubtedly a good point; on the other hand, countless times
over the years I've been asked by devoted Genesis fans, 'When
are you going to write down your side of the story?' My story is
that I met all the original members of the band at school, took
care of them through their formative years and saw them reach
unimagined heights of worldwide success. During these years we
all grew up together.

After 35 years in my second career as an energy consultant
I took retirement and thought, 'If ever there was a time to do
this book, it is now.' So it was that I plunged into the process of
reliving a treasure trove of memories, which, with the help of
writer Chris Charlesworth, morphed into the first draft of this
book. To my surprise, in telling this story, it extended beyond the
Genesis years, becoming a little more autobiographical. With that
in mind, I'll start at the beginning.

I was born in the English town of Bedford on September 17th 1950 but was conceived in São Paulo, south-east Brazil. My father had been posted there for his job after coming out of the army at the end of the war. I have never been to Brazil but maybe one day I will.

Both my parents came from Scottish ancestry and both were born in 1909; my father, David, in London and my mother, Mary, in Cardiff. Dad was a Scot whose family came from Mull. Macphail means son of Paul, Phail being Scottish Gaelic for Paul. My middle name is Paul, so I am Richard Paul, Son of Paul.

My mother had three sisters and a brother. One of the sisters had Down's syndrome and didn't live beyond her late teens, and my mother was the only one of the other three to get married. I had these two rather forbidding maiden aunts who looked after their father until he died and then, bizarrely, they fell out and never spoke to each other again.

There was this very strange custom in my family – I don't know how common it was for the time – but they all had three names. My mother was Ethel Mary but she was known as Mary and there was Doris Barbara and she was known as Barbara. When mum moved into a nursing home in Chichester they made a nameplate for her door that said Ethel Macphail and when we arrived to see her we saw the sign and thought, 'Who's this Ethel?'

My father worked for Vestey's, the big international food company, better known in the UK by the brand name 'Dewhursts the Butchers'; for his sins he was involved in chopping down rainforests and growing soya to feed cattle that wound up as roast beef on Sunday lunch tables back in England. I guess in those days no one cared much about the destruction of the rainforests but in today's enlightened age Dad might have had second thoughts as he was a man of principle, respectable, conservative, church-going and one of a rather stoic breed that in those days believed that a strong Britain was best for the world.

Dad had worked for Vestey's since before the war, during which he served with a Scottish Highland Regiment, ending up in North Africa and crossing over into Italy as the Allies pushed back the Germans towards the European heartland. He fought in the battles of Monte Cassino in 1944, a hard-won victory for the Allies that saw many casualties on both sides. He came away physically unscathed but never liked to talk about his war experiences. Many years later, my sister Moira's son, Andrew, was doing a school project about the Second World War. We were gathered as a family in the garden of a pub outside Chichester and Andrew started asking my father about his war experiences. Clearly overcome by the painful memories he nonetheless spoke about being at Monte Cassino. The thing that hurt the most was the memory of writing many letters to the wives and loved ones of those in his platoon who had been killed. That was more or less the only time I heard him talk about his war. How touching that it is often young people who bring out hitherto buried stories.

For part of the war Dad ran army training schools in Scotland and it was during this period that he met and married my mother, Mary Ward, in Northwood just outside London. My mother was a nurse and in 1941 she was posted on active duty to Freetown, the capital of Sierra Leone in West Africa. Dad was away for the first two years of my eldest sister Moira's life. Every week my mum would write letters to Dad in Scotland or wherever he was stationed but for some reason the letters all ended up in India. There was no other way of getting in touch, and they never worked out why their missives were sent there.

When the war ended Dad went back to work for Vestey's. My sister Kate was born in 1946, and I arrived four years later. They were all still in Brazil but my parents didn't want me to be born there, so in the summer of 1950 my mother came back early – on a boat as there were no planes to and from South America in those days. It turns out they were quite right as I might well have been made to serve in the Brazilian Army.

So my mother came back to live with her father who by then was retired and living outside of Bedford where I was born. Dad remained in Brazil with my two sisters, who were four and eight at the time and looking forward to having a little brother to look after.

Within a year of my birth my father came back from Brazil, never to return, and was given a job in Vestey's, London office in the City. We settled in Bramley, three miles south of Guildford, because my parents were impressed with St Catherine's, an independent Church of England school for girls that was located in the heart of the village. Kate was there from the ages of four until 16 when she went to Guildford Technical College, eventually becoming a teacher. Moira trained as nurse at Great Ormond Street in London.

We lived in a six-bedroom detached house on Links Road, with a golf course at the bottom of the garden. My father never had a mortgage and that big house cost him just £2000 in 1951, money he had saved up from working for Vestey's and living fairly frugally in Brazil. I suppose we were reasonably well off but not really rich. I know my parents made sacrifices to send the girls to St Catherine's, which was fee-paying. They would later do the same for me.

All through my youth I cycled around the lanes near where I lived, through Munster to Godalming, along the narrow byways that circled Bramley and down the road that leads to Guildford through Shalford, the village where I attended my first school, Ramsdean. I was there as a day boy, but when I was eight transferred to Aldro, a prep school in Shackleford where I was a boarder even though we lived only three miles away.

By this time Dad had left Vestey's and gone to work for Rank Hovis McDougall, another big food company, heading up their sales department. He was a great salesman, and I would inherit a bit of that from him as well as the good fortune he had in buying and selling property. As sales director, he ran the business nationwide, building up clients across the country with a fleet of van salesmen who went around all the housing estates.

The big thing in the world of bread at this time was a procedure known as the Chesham Method, which was a way of making white sliced bread that didn't need any kneading or proving. The whole industry was moving away from wholewheat bread and stodgy wartime stuff towards what the Americans called 'Wonderbread', the great bakery product of the age. Using a steam process, they came up with the ultimate tasteless pap: horrible white sliced fluff called Mother's Pride.

My dad commuted from Bramley to London every day. He had a little black Lambretta scooter and he would tootle off at seven in the morning, park it at Guildford Station and catch the train to Waterloo, then get on the Waterloo & City line to the Rank Hovis offices in the City. He sat in the same compartment with the same people on the same train every morning for years. They would give each other Christmas presents and knew all about each other's lives, what their wives were doing and where their children went to school.

As I've said, we weren't rich but Dad made a good living. We were on the right side of the divide. My parents made sacrifices to send me to prep school but that was because I was the boy. The girls attended a private school but as day girls since it was located only a five-minute walk away from where we lived. Being the boy, they had great aspirations for me to be a lawyer or a doctor or even a man of the cloth. Some hope.

I eventually grew to love Aldro but still remember the sound of young boys crying themselves to sleep in the dormitory at night. In that respect the regime was brutal. The fact that the school was near to where we lived didn't help. It might as well have been a thousand miles away because we couldn't go home no matter how close it was. Boys were allowed out on three Sundays per term, known as exeats, but not until the third Sunday when of course there'd be a general exodus. Later on I learned that the smart thing to do was not to go then as with only about 20 people left in the school you could get up to what you liked.

Over the years I spent quite a bit of time working out what happened to me emotionally, in my heart, at that school. At first I thought I'd been banished, abandoned, for something I'd done wrong. (I've done a bit of therapy in my life, including an American programme called EST (Erhard Seminar Training).) Even if I wasn't crying myself to sleep, some of the other boys in the dormitory were. Once one started he would set the others off until we were all crying, a dejected group of desperately homesick eight-year-olds missing their parents.

Those first few weeks were very difficult. Some of the boys, of course, came from miles away, including other countries. The tradition of those schools goes back to a time when families often used to be stationed in places like Africa or India and boys would be sent to their English boarding schools in September and there they would stay right through until the summer holiday of the following year. Your father would shake hands with you at the end of the summer and say, 'Bye bye son, we'll see you next July,' and that was it. In the holidays, Christmas and Easter, they would have a guardian.

Still, once I'd got over the shock of it all I settled into the routine of my prep school. The headmaster was called Crispin Hill, a man who cared deeply about the welfare of us boys. Like my parents he was a devout Christian. At home in Bramley we went to church every Sunday. It was the conservative thing to do – the Tory party at prayer, but of the good, caring kind. They were *Times* readers long before *The Times* was owned by Rupert Murdoch, they voted Conservative and they went to church every Sunday. Needless to say, this was not a path I followed in my own life.

The school grounds extended to some woods nearby and we would go there on Sunday afternoons and Mr Hill would build tree houses for us. Later, during my last term, another boy and I were allowed to sleep in the tree house, which at that age was a really exciting thing to do.

There was always some sport going on – you had to do it – but I never excelled. I was in the second XI for cricket and football. I wasn't brilliant academically either, just bumbled along in the middle. I was best at languages and geography because they interested me but struggled with maths and science. I was OK at English. I did once get an award for an essay I wrote about playing marbles. When it came to sitting the Common Entrance exam for my next school, Charterhouse, I needed to get 65%; I got 68%, so I always did just enough.

I went to Charterhouse in 1962. Although it is situated in Godalming, once more quite close to home, again I was a boarder. Founded by Thomas Sutton in Charterhouse Square in Smithfield, London in 1611, the school relocated and expanded to the Surrey town in 1872. Its motto is *Deo Dante Dedi* ('Because God gave, I gave') and, with its main building designed by Philip Charles Hardwick who designed the Great Hall at Euston Station, and its imposing position on a hill, remains the perfect embodiment of an English public school – oppressive, grand and in many ways a throwback to an age when the sun never set on the British Empire.

Charterhouse, of course, is where I first encountered the friends who would shape my life. But first I was in for a shock – as were they.

MY BOOK OF GENESIS

Chapter 2

MICK JAGGER –
THE DEVIL INCARNATE

*My sister gave me 'Teenager In Love' by
Marty Wilde for my ninth birthday. I woke up at three
in the morning and there it was, a brand new record by
the side of my bed. I wanted to play it, but thought
maybe there wasn't any electricity in the
middle of the night since everything
was switched off.*

Compared to my first two schools Charterhouse was enormous. It also had some weird traditions; for the first three weeks you were allotted someone called a 'father', a boy in the year above who would teach you the ropes and, hopefully, keep you out of trouble. Like all these sorts of schools you had to learn a lot of useless information. New arrivals were expected to be able to recite the names of the houses, all the names of the housemasters, who the head boy was, etc. After a few weeks you were tested and if you failed, your 'father' and you had to stand up on a table in the common room and sing a song in front of the whole rest of the house. (At Eton the system was even more extreme – if you did anything wrong your 'father' was beaten!)

So you had two lives. You had your life in the classroom with people your own age and then you had this parallel life with the people in your house who were all ages. And of course, because the place was so big – about 600 boys divided up into ten or twelve houses – you didn't know who most people were.

Our house was called Weekites. They were all something-ites, named after the master who had started the house, in our case the Reverend Weeks. This was where we slept, in great long dormitories, ten to a room, though when you were older you got a study. And then there was what is known in the public school system as 'fagging'. When you started you were what was called a 'running fag'. This meant that senior boys, the monitors – I think there were half a dozen of them – would come to the bottom of the stairs and shout 'FAAGGG' and you would have to drop whatever you were doing and run to them. The boy who arrived last got a job or an errand, as often as not going to the tuckshop at the top of the hill. 'Here's sixpence, get me some toffee,' they'd command, all very Molesworth stuff. Then you graduated to becoming a 'study fag' meaning your job was to get up in the mornings and clean up the monitors' studies. The monitors all had film posters up on their walls and were allowed a primus stove on which they would make food and you'd have to pick up the bits and pieces and clean the plates. Looking back on it now, it's a miracle the place didn't burn down.

We wore a school uniform that included a white shirt with a detachable stiff collar. The shirt would last you all week but you had to put on a new collar with studs and everything every day. At least we wore long trousers unlike at prep school where we wore shorts no matter what the weather was like. I remember that infamous winter of 1962/3 when it started snowing on Boxing Day and never stopped. It was wonderful as sport was cancelled but we still had to wear short trousers.

The first rule at Charterhouse was that you weren't allowed to cross the railway line without permission. The line was at the bottom of the hill and it separated the school from the town of Godalming and, a few miles away, Guildford. To cross the line you had to get a 'chit' from your housemaster, which wasn't forthcoming unless you had the best of excuses. I guess you could probably go 50 miles in the opposite direction but no one wanted to because there was nothing there. Of course, the idea was that it kept you out of whatever mischief you might get up to in town. The mischief we had in mind was to go to the record shop, find a booth and listen to the latest sounds. By now it was 1963 so what came to be known as the Swinging Sixties was all starting to kick off.

At home we had one of those enormous radiograms in our sitting room, not stereo, mono with one big speaker, a radio and a record player combined. My parents were music and theatre lovers. They'd go to Guildford, which had a fantastic repertory company, and also up to London to see musicals like *Oklahoma* and *Salad Days*. They would always buy the record of the show and whatever they brought back I would soak up like a sponge.

That all changed when my sister bought the first Stones' single 'Come On'. I can thank Kate for my introduction to pop music. When she was 16 she had an 18-year-old boyfriend who took her to see The Rolling Stones in Richmond. She was also into Cliff Richard but somehow we missed the first wave of American rock'n'rollers like Elvis and Little Richard. They passed us by. For Kate it was Cliff and Marty Wilde and Tommy Steele, the British equivalents of those Americans. Kate gave me 'Teenager In Love' by Marty Wilde for my ninth birthday. I got up at three in the morning and there it was, this record by the side of my bed. I wanted to play it, but I thought maybe there wasn't any electricity in the middle of the night since everything was switched off. When 'Come On', the first Stones single came into our house a couple of years later my mind was well and truly blown and I became a massive Stones fan, much more than The Beatles whom I learned to love much later.

Our mother hated the Stones and this, of course, was one of the reasons I loved them. Coming from her church background, she thought that Mick Jagger was literally the Devil incarnate. All that blatant sexuality and big lips and wiggling of hips was just too much for her; we would sit there watching them on this black and white TV and, well, the way Mum reacted made me love them all the more.

I suppose I should have guessed that I wasn't alone among the boys at Charterhouse to pick up on the sounds that were now dominating the charts. There were indeed others who shared my growing love for this music, and so it was that one Saturday afternoon during my first term I heard a rock band playing live for the very first time in my life.

I was near Hall, the main performance space with its proscenium stage where plays were put on and the whole school could assemble together, when I heard this live music coming through the wall. Naturally drawn to it, I entered through a side door and to my utter amazement there was a rock band practising. Later I learned they were called The Scarlet and the Black, a reference to *Le Rouge et le Noir*, a 19th-century classic psychological novel by Stendhal. Only at a public school would a band call themselves after a famous French novel!

I snuck in and watched them. The boys were two or three years older than me and, if they noticed my presence, they didn't seem to mind. Soon after I'd gone in they finished the number they were playing and put their instruments down to take a break. Evidently they had learned the habits of musicians early, you know... plenty of tea breaks!

They disappeared off somewhere and I stayed, looking at all the equipment, including a drum kit. Like many young men of my age I aspired to being a drummer. I even remember mentioning this to my father once and he said, 'Oh, you mean the timpani.' That was his only perspective. He had no idea what I meant. Anyway, there wasn't anyone around so a little audaciously I clambered behind the kit, picked up the sticks and just started playing. I knew the basics. You had the bass drum on your right, the hi-hat on the left, the snare between your legs and some cymbals and toms. (In a parallel universe I could have been a drummer because I've got quite a good sense of rhythm.) So there I was, bashing around making a horrible noise when unbeknownst to me a character who will soon become very important in this story heard what I was doing and thought that I made quite a reasonable sound.

His name was Rivers Maitland Alexander Job, or Rivers Job (pronounced as if it had an 'e' on the end, to rhyme with 'globe'). With such an unusual name it was only proper that he would be an unusual guy, unique in fact. He was the same age as me and I vaguely knew who he was since he was in my class. He came up and said he liked my drumming and told me that he had a band with a guy called Anthony Phillips with whom he had been at prep school, at St. Edmund's in Hindhead. Ant, as we would call him, hadn't actually arrived at Charterhouse yet; he was a little younger and would be coming next term.

Suddenly, the first time I sit behind a drum kit I've got a gig in a band! Richly undeserved, of course. Rivers, bless him, was the most extraordinary visionary who in time would introduce me to many amazing things, but as far as my drumming was concerned his judgement was a little off. He played bass and already had a Fender Precision, which was equally extraordinary; most professional groups, let alone boys of 13, could only dream about Fender basses.

At this stage my parents had moved to a cottage at Wotton on the road between Guildford and Dorking. This was Christmas Cottage, which would figure in the Genesis story before long. Apart from my sisters having left home, the main reason we moved to a smaller house was because my father had suffered a small heart attack and its location meant he would have to walk more, to get more exercise.

My parents bought the cottage from the brother of Bill Travers who starred with Virginia McKenna in *Born Free*, the famous film about adopting a lion cub in Kenya. Their name was Lyndon-Travers and they'd called it Christmas Cottage simply because they'd moved in one Christmas. My family used it as a weekend retreat; during the week they lived in a rented flat in Fetter Lane, off Fleet Street in London. The flat was in Clifford's Inn and, since it was my father's nature to often be disgruntled about things, he would write letters of complaint on his Clifford's Inn notepaper, which made people think he was a barrister.

This, of course, was the age when Fleet Street was the heart of the newspaper industry, with huge buildings occupied by the *Daily Express* and *Daily Telegraph*, where papers were printed on presses on the ground floors, and vans pulled away from the rear at all hours, delivering papers on which the ink was barely dry. As I became more and more interested in pop music I would go out on Wednesday afternoons and buy the latest edition of *Melody Maker*, newly delivered to the news stands on nearby streets, the first copies available anywhere in the UK. Then I'd ring my friends from Charterhouse and tell them all the latest pop news.

I soon learned that Rivers lived in London, in Park Street in Mayfair, with his mother and father, sister and brother, Charlotte and Crispin. It sounds very grand but it was actually Mr Job's business address. It was towards the end of my first term when he suggested we should get together in the holidays so I could be introduced to this Ant character who lived in Putney. Rivers gave me his phone number, which I can remember to this day: Mayfair 4209. Ant and I would always laugh about how his father answered the phone in his very posh voice.

Rivers and I arranged to meet up at Marble Arch and on the appointed day I got on the number 30 bus that went from Hackney to Roehampton, right past the end of Rivers's street to near where Ant lived. Rivers got on and we sat on the top at the front and watched London go by.

I hadn't been in the city long and London was still a bit of a mystery to me. We got off at the top of the hill in Putney and walked down this side street, past lines of huge detached houses. Ant lived in one with grounds, a tennis court and a swimming pool. My jaw hit the floor.

We went in and met Ant, a guy with very white blonde hair. There was an entrance hall and on the right a dining room. The antique oak dining table had been pushed to one side and the silk Persian rug rolled up, transforming the room into a rehearsal studio filled with equipment. Ant had a Strat – God knows how much that must be worth now – and there were amps and a rudimentary drum kit. Even more amazingly, his mum welcomed us into her home to play rock'n'roll music. Because my parents started their family quite late and I was the third child, they always seemed more like my friends' grandparents as far as their age was concerned, but Ant's mother was quite the opposite: a gorgeous young woman, probably aged about 35.

More importantly in view of what would follow down the line, whereas in my own household everything new in music was desperately resisted because of my mother's fear of Mick Jagger's hips and lips, here I was suddenly in a house where it was just the opposite, where it was positively welcomed. This family seemed only too happy that the dining room had been turned into a rehearsal studio. Ant, his mum and his aunt, even his grandmother, were all over us. 'Darlings it sounds wonderful,' they would say, even though the noise we were making was probably terrible. I was in a state of shock about all this; the contrast with my home was like night and day.

That day in Putney Ant played guitar and sang, Rivers was on bass and I sat behind the drums. I hit them as best I could but it soon became clear that my drumming was not up to scratch; it was not meeting the standard required by the others who were pretty good.

What saved the day for me was my sister's love of The Rolling Stones. The B-side of their second single, 'I Wanna Be Your Man', was called 'Little By Little', a sort of blues standard with a big harmonica solo in it. When my sister brought that record home I listened to it countless times and actually preferred the B-side to the A-side. I told them that I knew the words and without further ado, I was given the mic. When we'd finished, Ant very diplomatically suggested, 'Why don't you just sing? You're a much better singer than you are a drummer.' Needless to say I agreed. I remember doing this fake harmonica thing into the mic, doing the solo in 'Little By Little', and that clinched the deal. I became the singer.

Ant, of course, just blew my mind. He could play anything and he was only 13! His ear was incredible, his talent was giant. We would say, 'What about playing so and so?' and he could just play it. He was amazing for his age. It turned out that another guy from Charterhouse called Rob Tyrell, a great drummer, lived just around the corner, so he joined the next term and somehow – probably Rivers scouting again – we got a boy called Mike Rutherford on rhythm guitar and the as yet unnamed band was complete.

Michael John Cloete Crawford Rutherford, to give him his full name, boarded in another of the three houses going up the hill at Charterhouse. Weekites was the first, the next was Lockites, which was Mike's house, and the third one past the bridge at the top was called Girdlestonites. Apparently Mr Girdleston walked like a duck, so that house became known as Duckites. That was Anthony Phillips's house and also happened to be where two other boys, Peter Brian Gabriel and Anthony George Banks, lodged. Like all these new friends, they too would come to play a big and lasting role in my life.

As I got to know Peter and Tony through Ant I soon realised they were into pop music but they hadn't done anything about it yet. Actually they were already beginning to write stuff together but Ant was way ahead of everyone. Meanwhile, the advent of rock'n'roll, The Beatles and The Rolling Stones, the length of their hair and the clothes they wore, made not one iota of difference to life at Charterhouse. Like all such institutions, with its arcane rules and traditions it was stuck in the 19th century. The only house in the school that wasn't an 'ITE' was the original one, in the three-sided square, which was called Gownboys – all part of that strange language that your 'fathers' made you learn in the first three weeks. You could actually say to someone with a completely straight face: 'Grip me a tosh after homebill before banko.' That meant, 'Reserve me a bath after tea before prep.' There were whole sentences like that, as if we were some sort of secret society.

But to get back to what really mattered, Peter, Mike and Tony all arrived at Charterhouse in the same year as me, all of us born in 1950, but I didn't know them at first. Ant was actually a year younger than us. The boys I knew the best were those in my own house but I immediately became friends with Rivers, so from that point on we sat next to each other in class. I remember he had the most beautiful handwriting, like a medieval monk; much later he christened his daughter Rowan Maitland Alexandra Job, which sounds to me like a medieval woman's name. She lives in America nowadays but I'm in touch with her and she's so proud of her name. No question – Rivers Job changed my life.

MY BOOK OF GENESIS

Chapter 3

ANONYMOUS
AT CHARTERHOUSE

It seems ironic now that of all the boys in Anon,
the only one who would become a seriously
successful rock musician was the one
whose housemaster expressly forbade him
from playing the guitar.

I came up with a name for the group, Anon, like in a poem where the name of the poet is unknown. Somehow I just liked the idea of being anonymous and everyone agreed. It suited me that our line-up was the same as the Stones – two guitars, bass, drums and vocals – and slowly but surely the group came to dominate our lives. In Mike's words:

> *If you were into music it was a sort of natural linking up. It was like a sort of underground. There weren't many guys who were playing so we found each other.*

Mike was impressed with my singing. 'Rich was great,' he wrote in his book, *The Living Years*: 'He could sing, he looked good and he had all the moves.'

The attitude of the Charterhouse establishment towards the group was mixed. My housemaster was pretty relaxed about it, the Duckites housemaster was less so but Mike's housemaster, a man called Chare, known as Hacker Chare, hated it. He was an absolute bastard, a real sadist. As Mike wrote:

Hacker Chare banned me from playing my guitar. At the time I was in the upper house, a kind of recreation room, playing my guitar to Sgt. Pepper, which had just come out and was the most exciting thing I'd ever heard. Chare must have had a bad housemasters' meeting because he stormed in, raving, and grabbed me by the collar. 'Rutherford,' he hissed through his teeth, 'you are banned. You are not playing the guitar anymore.' He then bent me over and caned me. It was eight o'clock at night and I was in my dressing gown. After that, obviously, there was no way I was going to stop. Not least because the biggest concert of my Charterhouse career was only a few weeks away.

According to Anthony Phillips, it was well known at the time that Lockites was run by Hacker Chare on the same principle as a WW2 prisoner of war camp. He and Mike were constantly locking horns. He didn't like the idea that Mike even played the guitar, let alone owned one or was in a band. It seems ironic now that of all the boys in Anon, the only one who would become a seriously successful rock musician was the one whose housemaster expressly forbade him from playing the guitar.

The masters were known as beaks and we came to know which ones we could ask to use their classroom for a band rehearsal on a Saturday afternoon. We would borrow a trolley from the groundsman, pile the gear onto it and rumble our way across the cobblestones to certain classrooms, then set up and rehearse. Mike recently told me:

I remember the excitement of carrying the amps to rehearse. It was the highlight of my week. I didn't know much guitar to be honest, about four chords, but Ant became my mentor and showed me many more. Ant and I developed this two guitar thing which became the basis of early Genesis music.

We were well equipped: Ant had his Strat at the school along with a Vox AC30, the same amp used by The Beatles, and Rivers had his Fender Precision. The weak link in the gear was the PA so I was always the one who struggled to be heard. We would borrow one from somewhere, with two column speakers and a little amp, probably 50 watts. It's always the drummer who sets the volume because drummers can't really drum very quietly and everyone else has to go with them. In our set-up, the vocals seemed to get lost, even though I had quite a strong singing voice.

We started to get a few gigs, mostly at friends' parties, though I remember we did two concerts in the school grounds, both of them end of term 'hops'. Amazingly, we kept the same personnel together for three years, the only changes being forced on us when Mike lost his arguments with Hacker Chare and this other guy called Mick Coleman came in. Mike always borrowed a guitar belonging to his friend John Alexander, who's still a friend. He owned a Rickenbacker, for goodness sake, a six-string! John, bless him, had this amazing guitar but not a lot of talent. He did have all the gear though.

So we began getting gigs at parties during the holidays. Everyone lived in London, apart from Mike who lived in Farnham and whose father, Captain Rutherford, was a retired naval officer. Mike always managed to get to our gigs. One problem we had was our name because people couldn't cope with a band without the definite article. Instead of Anon people always called us The Anon. There's a picture of us performing at a dance at Rob Tyrell's house and his sister Marcia – a talented artist who we all fancied – had written The Anon on his bass drum.

Our repertoire was all cover versions, mostly Stones covers complete with Chuck Berry solos lifted note for note from the records. I loved their album *Out Of Our Heads* and, having now read the Keith Richards book *Life*, know that Andrew Oldham locked Mick and Keith in the kitchen of their flat in Kilburn and wouldn't let them out until they'd written a song. That was how they started writing their own stuff. The first song they penned together was 'As Tears Go By' which was recorded by

Marianne Faithfull; then there was another song called 'Blue Red and Grey' that Oldham got Cliff Richard to cover. It took the Stones a long time to come up with 'The Last Time' but it didn't take Ant long to produce some originals for us. He was the first of all of us to write serviceable songs, one of which led to our first and only recording.

There was a studio on Dryburgh Road in Putney called Tony Pike Sound. We pooled our cash and booked an hour there. We packed all the equipment into Ant's mum's Mercedes and got the bus down the hill to the studio. She was still really supportive (quite the opposite of my own parents, I have to say), delivering the gear for us. We reached the studio and I remember thinking that if the song was about three minutes and we had 60 minutes booked, we should be able to record three or four songs in the session. Of course, we just about got one song done, a song of Ant's called 'Pennsylvania Flickhouse' with nonsense lyrics. It's actually on YouTube.* I still have the original acetate from that session. Listening to it now, I hear what a complete Stones tribute/pastiche it is. For all that, not bad for a bunch of starry-eyed teenagers.

That recording was made in 1966 when I was 15. Of course, the group was now far and away the most important thing to me. This might explain why my school reports were so bad. My parents were shelling out all this money on my education and I would dread the day when the reports arrived because they were just getting worse and worse. The group was all I cared about but 'O' levels were fast approaching at the end of the summer term of '66, a situation that didn't bode well.

In the holidays we (me and my friends in the group) had started going to the Marquee in Wardour Street. I would meet up with them and read *Melody Maker* and go to Denmark Street to look at the guitars and amps in the windows, and then we'd head off to the Marquee. There was a band called The Action that we liked a lot and they were always supported by The Sands that we also

---

*https://www.youtube.com/watch?v=Wv691Av6Atc

really rated. I remember we saw Elton John as Reg Dwight when he was with Bluesology, playing a little Farfisa electric keyboard. In our undiscerning, adolescent way we thought he was a bit of a plonker because he was short and fat. How wrong could we be?

Another big favourite was The Jeff Beck Group with Rod 'The Mod' Stewart on vocals and Ronnie Wood on bass. Jeff is my desert island guitarist. I adore him and always have done. I love the tie-up between him and Stevie Wonder.

In Oxford Street there was another club called Tiles, across the road from the 100 Club. We used to go there and we even got into the Speakeasy near Oxford Circus on Margaret Street, the music biz hangout for the stars. We were far too young, of course, and it was probably Rivers who got us in because he had a lot of front even if he was quite short. We were there one night when John Lennon came in. We were sitting at a table and, as he came past to go to the loo, he went 'Hi' and we were just floored. I remember that we saw Skip Bifferty there and once Jimi Hendrix turned up.

Back at Charterhouse the head of music was a teacher called Geoffrey Ford and at the end of the summer term, we asked him if we could put on a concert. Geoffrey agreed to sort of sponsor us and it was made compulsory for all the boys in the school to attend, like a production of *Hamlet* or something, so we had a pretty big audience. There were three bands on the bill and we each did two sets with Anon closing. The third band was The Garden Wall, which included Peter Gabriel and Tony Banks. Ant played guitar with them as well as us. I guess it was a side project – he really was ahead of his time. Chris Stewart, the first drummer in Genesis, another Duckite, was in The Garden Wall as well so it was really a very early version of Genesis. Peter sang and Tony played a grand piano that was too big to fit on the stage so he had to be down on the floor. Still, it was four of the original Genesis in one band even if one of them was down a level! Tony recalls:

Nobody knew I was there until I did the introduction to 'When a Man Loves a Woman' and they were all going, 'Where's that coming from?' I also remember that one of the pieces we did was a 12-bar, which was just improvisation. I was just tinkling along playing chords, which was fine by me. But then we wanted to end it, and we couldn't catch Chris's eye to stop it, so it just went on and on and on. It went round and round and round, and I thought, 'Oh God, here we go again.' It was pretty bad.

Unlike Anon, however, The Garden Wall hadn't done much rehearsing so they were a bit loose. They hadn't done as many gigs as us either, hence we were top of the bill.

By this time I had noticed that Peter Gabriel, like Rivers, was someone who stood out from other boys. On the one hand, he was ridiculously shy and a bit of a mumbler but on the other hand, he completely knew his own mind. The first time I really became aware of him was at another hop where Anon was playing and he turned up with a girlfriend. To have a girlfriend was pretty much unheard of for boys at Charterhouse. The school was in some small way paired with my sisters' old school, St Catherine's, and among the girls to go there were Jill Moore and her sister Sally. It was Jill, like Peter aged 15, who came to the hop with him. The girls from St Catherine's would come over to Charterhouse for things like choir recitals and we'd be standing there watching them get off the bus with our tongues hanging out. I guess Peter must have met her through some school event.

As if having a real live girlfriend wasn't enough, Peter and Jill had somehow got hold of this enormous clear plastic bag and been through lots of people's front gardens, taken all the rose petals off their roses and stuffed them into it. This was 1966, almost before the beginning of flower power and when they arrived at the hop they spread rose petals all over the floor. We all got down on our hands and knees in it, so it was a bit of a happening.

Peter had an imagination way beyond mine. Not only did he have a gorgeous girlfriend – whom he later married – but he was into flower power before it even happened. Also, he had designed a hat like a pilgrim's – tall but not quite so pointed at the top – and taken the design to Locks, the hatmakers in London, and had

100 made which he sold. He was wearing one of these hats at the concert where The Garden Wall and Anon played. I always thought that to design a hat and have it made was pretty unusual for a boy of 15 or 16. But that was Peter – pretty unusual. He still is.

As for myself, I'd sent off by mail order for a pair of white bell-bottom jeans and there's a picture of us from this gig with me wearing them on stage. There's Rivers dwarfed by his enormous bass. People who didn't know what they were talking about were constantly telling him to get a smaller sized instrument.

At first the gig was great. We were playing 'Drive My Car' from The Beatles' *Rubber Soul* LP and 'Mister You're a Better Man Than I' by The Yardbirds. Then it all went pear shaped. Having been to the Marquee I'd seen how singers used to announce their songs and chat between numbers and I wanted to do the same thing. Apart from anything else I was proud of Ant's songs and wanted to introduce them, to tell the audience that Ant had written them. But Geoffrey was frightened that I would start a revolution and banned me from making any announcements between songs. Coming from a classical music tradition he wasn't fond of hearing any chat between numbers.

It just so happened that there was a technical glitch before we were going to do our penultimate song, 'Pennsylvania Flickhouse', something to do with a lead, and while some guys who were helping us with the technical side of things were sorting it out I made an announcement. Big mistake. At the end of 'Pennsylvania Flickhouse', our first record of which we were so proud, Geoffrey pulled the plug. 'That's it,' he said. 'You defied me. It's the end of the concert.'

We may have played live a few times but we had no idea how to build a set and the last song we'd planned to do was a cover of The Small Faces' version of Otis Redding's 'Shake'. We'd been down to the record shop in Godalming and got the guy in the shop to play it twice and that was enough for Ant to figure out the chords. I think we'd gone through it roughly once but it was hopelessly under rehearsed. Once Geoffrey had pulled the plug it all ended as a bit of a damp squib, but in hindsight he did us a bit of a favour because a really dodgy version of 'Shake' would have been a real anticlimax with which to end the show.

Of course it will come as no surprise that my mother did not like those white trousers one little bit. I made the mistake of leaving them at home during the following holidays when we went off on some camping trip and she burnt them. Put them on the bonfire. Unbelievable! There I was, top of the bill, the singer with the best band in school and loving it and then I get home and they hate everything about it. My mum was the government and dad was the police force. And of course the reports were coming in and they were just… Well, suffice to say, it was terrible at home.

Things. Would. Have. To. Change.

Chapter 4

THE WILDERNESS YEARS

While I was there I kept seeing Keith and Mick roll up in this filthy old Bentley and Brian would tumble out, clearly stoned out of his head.

And change they did.

I was 16 and had taken and failed most of my 'O' levels, a state of affairs my mother and father not unreasonably blamed entirely on the insidious lure of rock'n'roll music. Along with Rivers, clearly an unsuitable role model, I was to leave Charterhouse and resume my studies elsewhere while the rest of our friends stayed on. As a result Anon collapsed, Mike and Ant got together with Peter, Tony and Chris and – drum roll, please – Genesis, as they would become known, was born.

Needless to say, it wasn't quite as simple as that and a lot would happen in the lives of us all in the coming year. Rivers's parents decided that he would do better at a crammer, so they sent him to one in Notting Hill, a famous (or infamous) establishment called Davis Lang & Dick. That didn't seem to help so, to digress a little, he eventually graduated into the world of blues, ending up as the bass player in The Savoy Brown Blues Band. So there he was, still this tiny guy with a bass too big for him, playing with Savoy Brown, a 'name' band right in the thick of the British blues boom. One evening he dragged me to see John Mayall & the

Bluesbreakers at the Ram Jam Club in Brixton where Eric Clapton could be found playing lead guitar right at the time they were recording the famous *Bluesbreakers* album featuring Eric on the cover reading the *Beano*. We were lucky to hear all of those songs live before the album came out.

Sadly Rivers's path to success didn't last. He simply took too many drugs and blew his mind, ending up with a debilitating mental illness and eventually committing suicide. At the age of 29, he was found on a railway line in West London. The inquest recorded death by misadventure. It was a terrible loss. He was one of those casualties with whom we became all too familiar. A lot of us took acid but not to the extent that Rivers did; he'd take it before gigs and that cost him his place in Savoy Brown. He became hopelessly unreliable and they booted him out.

Horrendously, I found out later from his sister Charlotte that both his father and his brother also killed themselves – three men from the same family, a strange and tragic family theme. All that crazy flair that I loved about Rivers had a downside that I only later came to accept. We'd stayed in touch through the 70s, in the midst of which I found myself involved in opening up a whole street of squats in Freston Road, North Kensington. Rivers moved in but he wanted to be close to the earth, so he tore up all the floors of the house he was living in so he could sleep on the ground, on the earth. Something had gone very wrong with him. He was living there when I heard that he had died. I'd gone to see Peter Gabriel playing in the South of France and when I came back heard the terrible news.

But to return to 1966... I wasn't actually kicked out of Charterhouse, though that's what many of my friends thought. I was on the list of boys who would return to take their 'O' levels again, a system called the White List, and was due to go back in the autumn term. I would have returned, gone down a year and retaken 'O' levels but in the interim, like Rivers, I went to a crammer, this one in Gloucester Road in South Kensington. It was called Carlisle & Gregson, for some reason known as Jimmy's.

There was no normal school structure at these places, no sport or any other activities. You just went and crammed for exams, which is what I did from the autumn of 1966 to the spring of '67.

The great thing I remember about this crammer was that it was around the corner from where Brian Jones of the Stones lived in Courtfield Gardens and where, famously, he was busted for drugs. While I was there I kept seeing Keith and Mick roll up in this filthy old Bentley and Brian would tumble out, clearly stoned out of his head. In Keith's book *Life* he writes about the time when Brian was living there with Anita Pallenberg. Keith fell in love with her too; he would come across from where he was living in Hampstead, often walking all the way to Gloucester Road, and spend several days there just to be around Anita whom he eventually nicked from Brian. All this was happening just across the road from where I was supposed to be studying. Of course, much of the time I'd be hanging out on the street waiting to catch a glimpse of them.

At the time, I was staying in Clifford's Inn on Fetter Lane with my parents and going by bus to Gloucester Road every day. In reality I can't have spent too much time watching out for stray Rolling Stones as I retook my exams and passed them all. The crammer must have worked because as well as the two or three 'O' levels I got at Charterhouse I gained four or five more, though without maths which I never achieved, even after taking it seven times! There is an irony there – many years later I became an energy efficiency trainer, a job for which you need quite a lot of maths, and so I found myself successfully teaching a subject that I had struggled so much with earlier. I always used to say to the slower trainees, 'If I can understand this then I know that you can.'

Next, armed with my impressive new credentials, I was dispatched to another, even more expensive private school, Millfield in Street, Somerset, where I went straight into the 'A' level stream. Like Charterhouse, it was a famous school, founded in 1935 by Jack Meyer in a house originally owned by the Clark family, shoe manufacturers, which is the other thing for which Street is famous. In 1939, Millfield became one of the first independent schools to become co-educational, meaning girl trouble though it wasn't 50/50 male to female. There was one house with about 50 girls and all the rest were boys, about 500 of us.

This was another strange move for me because when I tell people I went to Millfield they always assume I must have been good at sport. The school has this reputation because so many famous sports stars went there; they include the rugby player, Gareth Edwards, the swimmer, Duncan Goodhew and Gold medal winning Olympic rower, Helen Glover. Jack Meyer was a very charismatic and visionary man whose abiding principle was that every person is good at something, therefore, as educators, you take that something and encourage it to Olympic level. The rest will take care of itself. At least, that was the theory.

The other notable aspect of the school was that in order to pay for it all, he had to attract the sons or daughters of the wealthy. Elizabeth Taylor's son Michael Wilding was there because he'd been struggling with his studies – perhaps not surprising coming from that family. His parents would have gone to Jack and asked if he'd take their son and he'd say, 'Of course,' with open arms, but at three times the normal fees. The people who could afford it would pay a lot of money to send their children to Millfield. Many celebrities' kids went there, among them Lew Grade's nephew Philip Black, still a good friend of mine, actor Stanley Baker's daughter and Haile Selassie's grand-daughter, Mariam Asfa Wossen… a whole mixture of people with interesting back stories. So it was a blend of brilliantly talented sports people from poor backgrounds and troubled rich teenagers all mixed together. I suppose that I was somewhere in the middle.

Like Charterhouse we were all divided up into houses, but unusually these were spread around the Somerset countryside, some bigger than others, some purpose built. Mine was called Mill House with only 15 boys while Kernick down the road housed only eight.

We'd all be rounded up in the morning and taken to the school in a fleet of buses. Ours was a red pre-war vehicle called the Dorsal Fin (sometimes you see them in old films), which really did have a fin as well as a huge sunroof. It was a lumbering old bus, built like a London single-decker but with a separate cab for the driver. Our driver was Scottish and so naturally, we called him Jock. Not terribly original I know.

Mill House was on the River Brue. Each morning we would see the bus emerging out of the mist, coming round the corner over the bridge, and we'd all shout 'Jock' at the top of our voices and get ready to leap on board. Jock was almost certainly an alcoholic. He would be driving around, pissed as a newt even first thing in the morning, so it was clearly absolute madness entrusting all these kids to him.

The route to school took us through the village of Barton St David where there was a T-junction. On the corner was the garden of a family with a boy who probably had cerebral palsy or some sort of mental health issues. Somebody christened him 'Happy' because he was always really thrilled to see us. The red bus would appear and he would run down the garden as it went around the corner really slowly, lick his hands and smear them on the bus window. We'd all go 'Eurrrgggh!' But Happy would be remembered, as we shall see.

There was one last pick-up to make for two day boys who lived at home. Their names were Anthony and David Corey-Wright and Jock's aim always was to try and skip picking them up if he could possibly help it. Most days they'd be dutifully waiting by the side of the road so he would stop, but it was by a straight stretch; Jock would have the bus going at full speed, probably only about 40 miles an hour, and we'd all be leaning out the back as they came running out of the house. We'd all yell, 'Jock!' and he would have to stop to pick them up as they came running down the road. Many years later I found myself sitting next to someone called Jane Corey-Wright at an EST seminar – it was Anthony and David's mum. I told her that story and she laughed her head off.

We'd then arrive at the school and all pile out. The first thing I always looked for was whether or not the inflatable tent that housed the swimming pool was standing. Swimming was the only sport I did at Millfield but I didn't particularly like it, so I'd be hoping it would have blown down, as so often happened, and the session be cancelled. So much for my sporting prowess.

I was at Millfield for my 'A' Levels but after a year my results didn't improve. The idea was that I would study English Literature, History and Geography. I was also doing music 'O' level, which involved studying theory and set pieces. One of these was Bach's Italian Concerto for harpsichord, a piece that taught me to love his music. Quite a departure from the Stones but one that captivated me. There was also Mozart's Linz symphony while our third piece was *A Ceremony Of Carols* by Benjamin Britten for boy treble voices and a harp. This sudden immersion in classical music would serve as an important piece of the jigsaw of my musical life. Little did I know that I would end up marrying a professional harpsichordist.

As at Charterhouse, I knew everyone in my house and everyone in my various classes, but hardly any of the rest of the boys and girls, most of whom were younger than me. Although there were two blocks of modern classrooms, as often as not the classroom was a Nissen hut, what Americans called a Quansit hut, temporary buildings made from corrugated iron and bricks that were freezing cold in the winter and boiling hot in the summer, with nothing in between. There were only five or six in a class meaning that we had a huge number of teachers. Everyone was paying stacks of money to be there, to have this kind of education, with the focus that small classes offered. At the time, Charterhouse cost £3000 or £4000 a year and Millfield twice that. It makes my eyes water to think what they must cost now.

There was quite a bit of interaction with the girls, but no intercourse of course. I remember best a girl called Vivienne Merson whom I really fancied and who, much to my astonishment, seemed to like me. As a teenager I was very much of the Groucho Marx school: I'd never want to be a member of a club that would have me as a member. I was convinced that no girl would ever find me attractive and was very unsure of myself. That is, until I met Viv.

I'll never forget the moment when Viv Merson and I clicked. There was a sort of club room where you could go in the breaks between classes, with a slot machine that sold bars of chocolate and a juke box that, thrillingly, had all the current hits loaded into it. That day there was a crowd of people in a circle and I joined it. Viv was there and I looked at her and smiled and she smiled back, and it was like the proverbial bolt of electricity shot through me. Wahey! I also remember her friend Sally who was a 'pocket rocket' and much fancied by everyone. These two beautiful girls would get off the bus from their house and hide in a Nissen hut and wait for me to come along. They didn't even know my name at first, but they decided to call me Alistair because I had red hair and looked Scottish.

In fact, I was a very spotty red-headed teenager, freckly, covered in acne, so I thought I was hideously unattractive but apparently Viv could see beyond that. We got together at a hop one Saturday night. In no time we were round the back of one of the Nissen huts and having a lovely snog. There weren't enough girls to go around so I was very lucky to find one and from that night onwards it was always Viv, Sally and me walking through the school from the coach park together.

In spite of the thrill of forming a relationship with Viv, something strange was also happening. As much as I wanted to be close to her I was, at the same time, overcome by a strong sense of terror. Many years, many seminars, many hours of therapy later, I now feel able to make some sense of what was going on. I was deeply hurt by my mother when I was sent away to boarding school aged eight. Later, in my teenage years, when I began to grow close to Viv, I felt unconsciously that I was going to get hurt again. It made it very hard for me to commit myself beyond a certain point. Of course, I was completely unable to articulate this to Viv. As a result, sadly, our love just fizzled out.

Just like at Charterhouse, I formed a band at Millfield with, among others, a chap called Harry Williamson whose father,

Henry Williamson, wrote *Tarka the Otter*. We mostly played blues. Again I was the vocalist, Harry was the guitarist, there was a guy called Ian on guitar and two others who played bass and drums. We called ourselves The Austin Hippy Blues Band because someone found out that the kid we called Happy was really called Austin, like the A30 car, so we honoured him by calling our band after him. The height of our brief career was when the Bishop of Bath & Wells, in an attempt to reach out to the youth of the day, organised a local band competition at his palace. We all played in a big room there and our band won. Somebody actually decided that we were the best. Heaven knows why… maybe because we all had great shoes. Clark's had a seconds shop in the town and one of the styles they made were desert boots which were cool and you could buy for next to nothing.

I got my music 'O' level at Millfield but that was all, so my parents wisely decided to stop throwing good money after bad. They let go of their dreams of me becoming a lawyer or a doctor or doing something worthwhile and took me away after the spring term of 1968, obviously tearing their hair out wondering what to do with their hopeless failure of a son who just kept wanting to do rock'n'roll.

And they decided to send me as far away as possible.

My parents David and Mary Macphail on their wedding day in May 1941. My father got special leave from his Scottish regiment for the day.

With my sisters Kate and Moira at our house in Bramley, Surrey in the mid 50s.

Singing with Anon
at Charterhouse in the
summer of 1966.

Rivers Job is the
bass player.

This is the cover of the CD single of 'Pennsylvania Flickhouse' issued by
the German Genesis fan club. The photo shows Anon playing at a private
party in 1966.

Rivers Job, Rob Tyrell, Mike Rutherford, Anthony Phillips and RPM

Peter and Jill's wedding at St James's Palace.
From left: Fred Munt, Tony Stratton-Smith, RPM, Steve Hackett & Gail Colson

At Peter and Jill's wedding.
From left:
Mike Rutherford with his girlfriend Josie, Robin with John Alexander, RPM and John Anthony's foot.

Sport Palace outside Turin with the truck backed up to the stage and RPM mixing the sound at bottom left.

Working in the back garden at Freston Road in 1976 – thank you Tony Sleep for the photo.

Chapter 5

EYELESS IN GAZA

---

*Thank God my parents didn't know
what I was really up to.*

Meanwhile, back at Charterhouse my friends were busy writing songs. It was their song writing that brought them together to form the group that would become Genesis. Anthony Phillips remembers:

> *Mike and I were beginning to write songs together and we thought that the music would benefit from the addition of a piano player. I was in the same house as Tony Banks so I asked him if he would like to work with us. He said that he'd be pleased to but that he would like to include Peter Gabriel as they had also started writing songs togther and that Peter was showing the early signs of becoming a good singer. So we said yes, by all means. So as young songwriters together we pooled our resources.*

So – please forgive the pun – this was the genesis of Genesis. Thanks to the technical skills of another Charterhouse boy, Brian Roberts, a demo tape, including songs by both pairs, was duly recorded.

Meanwhile, through Reeds Employment Agency, I had taken a temporary job as a messenger for a firm of stockbrokers in the City, picking up big cheques and delivering them to and from offices and banks. One of the streets where I plied this trade was called Poultry, near the Bank of England and Cheapside and on it was a record shop where I bought 'The Silent Sun' on the very day it was released. I distinctly remember that it was a Thursday, the same day that an edition of *Melody Maker* went on sale in which Chris Welch actually reviewed it in his singles column. 'Dear Jonathan King,' he wrote, 'you have released upon the world a work of such…' and he went on to slag it off and then rebuked himself in a pastiche of Shakespeare: 'Zounds man, I'm jesting, 'tis sorry sport to make satirical pokes at one of the better sounds of the week.' Then he went on to describe the record, saying it had 'Peter Frampton-ish vocals'. Funny that, everyone else thought it sounded like The Bee Gees what with Peter quivering like Robin Gibb and the rest of them joining him for a chorus.

How all this came about is writ large in the Genesis legend. Another old Charterhouse boy was the slightly eccentric Jonathan King who was quite a bit older than us. He'd had a hit single in 1965 with 'Everyone's Gone To the Moon', so he bought a sports car and came back to the school on an Old Boys' day as a returning hero. John Alexander, the guy with the Rickenbacker, gave him a copy of the demo and King evidently liked Peter's voice. As Ant recently told me, 'It was Peter's voice and one of Tony and Peter's songs that clinched the deal for King.'

Pursuing his belief in their potential, he signed them to Decca where he was working as an A&R man, moving from being a pop star to recording other people. Jonathan King has recently been in the news again after being convicted for having sex with teenage boys. He received a seven-year prison sentence in 2001 and was paroled in 2005.

It was perhaps fortunate that the five boys in the group were all under 18 because they signed an appalling contract, a familiar story with naïve young musicians. They might well have been stitched up to this day. So it was that the original Genesis – Peter Gabriel, Tony Banks, Mike Rutherford, Anthony Philips and Chris Stewart – went on to record the album that became known as *From Genesis To Revelation*. It was King who named them

Genesis because for him, if not for them, it was the beginning of a new career phase. The recording of the album, which, unlike the single, wouldn't be released until 1969, all happened while I wasn't around. Though I would stay in touch with them and their adventures through letters, it would be a good while before I rejoined their story.

When all of this was happening, I was 2,236 miles away, the distance between Guildford in Surrey and Ashkelon in Israel where, in a final, desperate move, my long-suffering parents sent me to a kibbutz in order to 'find myself', a place where they knew I would be looked after and which would broaden my horizons. They were quite right in that respect and in hindsight, it was an inspired move even if it utterly failed to quench my thirst for rock'n'roll music.

It was in the spring of 1968 that my sister Kate had befriended a girl who'd gone to work on a kibbutz. Back then Israel was a profoundly left-wing country populated by Jewish people who'd come from various parts of Europe with nothing to their name but the clothes on their back. Seeking a fresh start and a home that they could call their own after the horrors of the Holocaust, they arrived keen to join the kibbutz movement. The government had formed these communities (known as *kibbutzim*) where people were provided with everything they needed to survive and prosper: housing, food, clothes, work and, perhaps most important, companionship with others in the same boat.

Although our family wasn't Jewish I was able to enter the system and become a volunteer, so they fixed up for me to go to a kibbutz called Zikkim on the coast, just south of a town called Ashkelon, not far from Gaza.

The only way to get there in those days was by sea, so after crossing the English Channel I took a train down through France to Marseille and caught a boat owned by the Israeli shipping line *Zim*. It was a cruise ship, stopping at cities en route to Israel: Genoa, Naples, Athens and Limassol in Cyprus. We'd sail during the night and embark at these ports during the day for trips ashore. To an untravelled lad of just 17 this was all eye poppingly exotic.

It was the first time I went up Vesuvius, an experience which ignited a life-long fascination for all things volcanic.

Eventually I arrived in Haifa. I was travelling completely on my own. Had I been wiser, I'd have taken a bus to the kibbutz, which would have cost me next to nothing. However, I was a little overwhelmed by the transport system and climbed into one of those big American cars called Cheroots, a sort of cross between a bus and a taxi. The driver took me the whole way but in the meantime kept stopping and picking people up and detouring around Tel Aviv. He spoke some English and I ended up paying him £30, an absolute fortune, all the money I had. But I did get there safely.

It was quite a small kibbutz and one of the reasons my parents chose it was because it was mostly English people who had settled there. Obviously Israel was keen to attract lots of people to their country. It was a year after the Six Day War and in order to keep up the defence of the country, they had a system where most people, whatever they did, were also in the armed forces. When the Six Day War broke out everyone dropped everything and went to fight. Answering a call, masses of Jews from the entire Diaspora came in to drive the taxis, harvest the crops and do all of the jobs that the soldiers would have done – all volunteers. Even though the war ended very quickly, many of them stayed on and by the time I arrived, had been there for nine months simply because they liked the way of life.

I spent six months at the kibbutz, from April to September 1968, and met many amazing people in our little compound. I was hugely impressed with the kibbutz system. It seemed to me, at my idealistic age, that this communal model, true socialism at work, made total sense. I was especially impressed by the way the children were cared for. If you had a child it would go first to the baby house, where it would looked after by both its mother and other young men and women, specially trained in child care. Gradually these pods of children, all the same age, would grow up together. I know this style of child-raising has become very controversial but at the time, like so many other aspects of kibbutz life, it seemed close to ideal.

Kibbutz Zikkim had the most beautiful gardens. I picked fruit, worked in the dairy, made breakfast for the community and operated the grain-cleaning machine. The volunteers were supposed to do six hours' work a day and two hours of Hebrew but the Hebrew lessons had fizzled out before I arrived. After starting work very early, we had a lot of time on our hands. Most people were there with a view to staying but not me. I suppose I might have stayed but I knew that if I did, like everyone else, I would have had to go into the army, something I did not want to do because, you know, 'I was a hippy, man.'

For our labours we were given 50p a week. Everything you needed was provided: toothpaste, airmail letters, food and clothing. We wanted for nothing. We would save up our 50ps and take a bus into Gaza (occupied Egypt) and buy Lebanese gold hashish. That's where I learned the joys of smoking dope.

The volunteers all smoked hash. We didn't flaunt it but nor did we hide it. It was highly illegal and probably unbelievably dangerous going into Gaza to score from our dealer, Abdul. He would give us raw poppy extract, opium to you and me, in the hope that we would get addicted, so we used to make joints with a mix of opium and hashish. We were reckless. Zikkim was right near the sea, a gorgeous setting, but we weren't supposed to go there because there were unexploded mines on the way to the beach. Later on, right towards the end of my time there, a path was cleared and on Saturdays, our day off, we would all go down to the beach. Prior to the path being cleared, we would walk across the dunes, very stoned, without a care in the world, crazy and stupid but it was a fantastic time. Thank God my parents didn't know what I was really up to.

My only contact with England was by letter, so I wrote to my parents and to Ant, who filled me in on what Genesis was up to during the summer of 1968. Mostly they were practising and composing, but with no live gigs to speak of. During this time, they released a second single called 'One Eyed Hound' which surprisingly, I managed to pick up on the radio at the kibbutz. The only music I could get on the radio was the British Forces

Overseas station broadcast from Cyprus and when they played 'One Eyed Hound' one Saturday morning I made sure everyone knew. 'Those are my friends!' I yelled, but I don't think anyone believed me.

It may come as no surprise that the reason I left the kibbutz was because I was busted. I could sense a political change going on, following an election of the kibbutz governing committee. It seemed to shadow what was going on in the Israeli government at the time. There was a shift to the right on matters of defence and the new committee was concerned that we volunteers from other countries would infect the young Israelis with our hippy ways, our joints and long hair. They were completely wrong, of course. It would have happened anyway in the liberal atmosphere of the kibbutz. I remember the bust happened just after I had lost my virginity to an Australian girl. I was 17 and she was 27. Her name was Connie and she kind of helped herself to me. I didn't complain.

The committee had warned us that they were going to inform the police about the dope smoking so we cleaned the place out. Unfortunately one of the guys, a real committed drug taker called John from Bolton (if he's still alive now it'll be a miracle) didn't do a good enough job. The Lebanese gold that we favoured came in bricks that were wrapped in cotton material and sliced up into what they called fingers. John had bought half of one of these bricks but although he got rid of the hash he forgot to throw out the wrapping. It still had residue on it, so when the police came and searched the place the traces of our beloved pastime were found.

John, Martin and I were all arrested. It seemed arbitrary, but maybe my very long hair had something to do with my being included. They wanted to make an example of us. We were taken to Ashkelon and put in a police station called a Tegart Fort, one of hundreds that the Brits had built all over the Empire. This one was designed to hold Israeli terrorists, or freedom fighters depending on your point of view. We were held there for three days but all in all, were quite well treated. The cell walls were covered in graffiti, smeared on with shit but it didn't smell. It was all in Hebrew so we couldn't read it anyway. They fed us, gave us a bucket, and we just hung out and slept and told each other our life stories. Occasionally some guy would be thrown in with us before being hauled off somewhere. When we were bailed out and went back to the kibbutz we were treated like returning heroes. The women were all over us!

A few weeks later the three of us went to Beersheba for a court appearance and were each fined 50p. I knew it was time for me to leave Israel, so I retraced my steps, back to Haifa, back on the boat, across the Mediterranean to Marseille and through France to England. I thought there might have been a sequel to this many years later when I travelled to Israel with my wife Maggie who often plays concerts there. Thirty years had passed and at the passport control I was worried they would find my criminal record and not grant me an entry visa but they didn't. Clearly the records from 1968 hadn't made it onto their computer.

MY BOOK OF GENESIS

Chapter 6

THE COTTAGE

'I think we would have killed each other without Rich.'
Mike Rutherford

It was October 1968 and had I been one for listening at keyholes I'm pretty sure the sole topic of my parents' conversation would have been, 'Oh my God, what are we going to do with him now?' I was back at Clifford's Inn in Fetter Lane, off Fleet Street, my prospects as short as my hair was long, my appetite for hashish as great as it had been in Israel, my immediate future as void as that to which John Lennon encouraged us to surrender in 'Tomorrow Never Knows'.

But I was nothing if not resourceful. My mother owned a sewing machine and thanks to this I began to scratch out a basic living making leather jackets with tassels that I sold at Kensington Market. My friend Michael Reed had made leather shoulder bags with requisite fringes on the bottom, the big ones that held 12-inch albums which he sold at Biba. I adapted his idea, stole it really. I got my leather from a Greek guy called Giorgos who had a shop in Tottenham Street and would sell me offcuts from which I would fashion waistcoats. I'd typically make five or six in a week and take them to Kensington Market on Saturday mornings. The stallholders would give me £5 for each one and sell them at double the price. They'd usually be all gone by lunchtime, so I made £25 minus my costs. I'd give a fiver to my mum for my board and lodging and keep the rest. Since half an ounce of hash was £4.50 in those days, I was laughing.

It would have been in the winter, probably December, when I made a drug connection in Edith Grove, though I can't remember how I figured out how to do it. Other than my trips to Gaza, this was the first time I'd scored hash in London. My contact turned out to be a hippy couple living in a basement, just off the Kings Road, not far from where the Stones' notorious early flat was. I'd get on the number 11 bus from Fleet Street, knock on the door and hand over my £4.50. As I walked out, the small foil-wrapped package would burn a hole in my pocket; I was convinced that everyone was looking at me and knew what I was carrying. I was probably paranoid because I'd have shared a joint with the couple while I was there – that was the ritual in those days – so I'd be standing at the bus stop in the snow imagining that a special patrol group van was following me back from Chelsea to Fleet Street.

At this time, my parents would go down to their cottage at Wotton at the weekend, leaving me alone in the flat. As soon as they left on a Friday evening, after the rush hour to avoid the traffic, I'd be on the phone to my friends giving the signal for all clear. We would proceed to have a riotous weekend at the flat, going out to the 24-hour Golden Egg in Fleet Street in the middle of the night because we were stoned out of our heads and had the 'munchies'. Our ritual included watching *Danger Man* with Patrick McGoohan late on a Friday night.

Another attraction for everyone was my stereo amp, made for me by my brother-in-law, John Firth, who had married Moira, my elder sister. He was a very clever and practical man, a scientist, who could build anything electronic. He's now a webmaster, building websites for people. Somehow it came up in conversation that I wanted a stereo amplifier, so he made me one from scratch. He bought all the bits, knew exactly what to do and successfully assembled and soldered it all together for me. I bought a turntable, a Garrard Lab 80, and took it to their home in Cambridge, along with some headphones and we got it all connected up. I also took with me Jeff Beck's *Truth* album, which opened with a cover of The Yardbirds' 'Shapes Of Things', a much heavier version. I put this on with the headphones and it was utterly mind-blowing, completely life changing for me. 'Oh my god,' I thought. 'This is how it was meant to sound.'

Of course I got some speakers too; in fact, I was the first person in the Genesis crowd to get a stereo. I would sit them down (they'd probably had a spliff or two) and watch in anticipation as the music started playing. It was so much fun to see their faces when they heard stereo on headphones for the first time and, of course, when someone is listening on headphones they completely forget themselves and start singing very loudly, usually way out of tune, or shouting when they want to talk to you. They would have heard stereo before because *From Genesis To Revelation* was released in both mono and stereo. I remember that in those days on Decca, a hole was punched in the outer LP sleeve and the inner sleeve was either red or blue, one for mono and one stereo, so you could see which it was when you slid the record in.

That first Genesis album was released in March 1969, recorded the previous year, partly when I was in Israel, but there was a long gap between recording and release. It died a death, of course. No promotion, no interest from the label – hopeless when you think about it and pointless too. Fortunately the boys weren't going to let something like this put them off. They were far too determined to believe that this was the end of the road.

At this time Tony Banks was at Sussex University and had a job working at Harrods while staying with us at Clifford's Inn. I now got to know him properly for the first time as I hadn't shared a house with him at Charterhouse. I discovered that he was a very quiet, shy, reserved guy but behind that mild exterior was someone who knew what he wanted and would stop at nothing to get it. He only stayed at our flat for a couple of weeks, over the Christmas vacation of 1968, but it was long enough for me to realise that, like the rest of them, Tony was unwavering in his motivation.

Meanwhile, Mike was still living at his parents' home in Farnham, Peter was at the family farm in Chobham and Ant was living at Send, near Woking, where his family had moved from Putney. It was an impressive house called Send Barns, set in its own extensive grounds. At this time Peter, with aspirations to become a film director, had enrolled in the London Film School. You have to wonder how that would have turned out. Talk about sliding doors... One of his favourite film directors was the surrealist Alejandro Jodorowsky and I remember him dragging me and Jill off to the Curzon Cinema in Mayfair to see a film called *El Topo*, a cult US-Mexican western drama, really an acid trip on film. Even though he had never taken acid that's the kind of film Peter liked, so you can imagine what he would have done if he'd become a director.

Oddly or perhaps predictably, Peter had bought an old London taxi to use as his car. There's a picture of them all standing by it: Peter, Mike, Tony, Ant and one of the drummers, probably taken at Ant's house or Peter's parents' home in Chobham, a farm called Deep Pool. Peter's father Ralph, who lived to be 100, only ever lived in Chobham his whole life. He was a quiet, reserved, shy man, an engineer and inventor. Ralph came up with the concept of sending a TV signal down the telephone line but his bosses couldn't see any future in it. Steve Jobs at Apple is said to have invented the mouse when he was working at Rank Xerox. He and his team went to his bosses and said this will make computers available to everyone but they said, 'Don't be silly, computers are only for big corporations. There will never be a time when everybody has a computer in their house.' It was a bit like that with Peter's father and the phone line. Why would people want to do that if they could get free television from the BBC?

Ralph's father had been a wealthy timber merchant and when he got married his parents gave him the farm, so for the first part of his life he lived with his parents and the second at Deep Pool. There was a private track leading to it from the road and while they were rehearsing there, I used to practice driving in Peter's taxi which had the heaviest steering imaginable. Power steering hadn't been invented. I didn't have a driving licence yet but I was off road so it was a good place to get some practice.

The attitude of the other Genesis parents towards the band was always very encouraging, unlike mine who hated the whole idea. I suppose I must have been wearing them down slowly but surely; their protests about my lifestyle were gradually withering into a kind of jaded acceptance. There I was making my leather jackets but quietly they must have been despairing over me. Only once did I have a real showdown with my father, when he expressed great frustration about where my life was not going. One thing that we never saw eye to eye on was the telephone. His generation had a completely different attitude to phones than my own. To them it was a sacred thing, meant only for emergencies, not for chatting. I couldn't take the phone into my bedroom so when I wanted to call Ant my father would say I could call him, but he would be putting the kettle on to make a cup of tea and when it boiled the call would have to end. This became a running joke between me and Ant: 'The kettle's boiling. I've got to go.' The phone was in the hall where it was draughty and cold and everyone could hear what you said. I'm sure my mum and dad weren't alone in their strange reluctance to embrace the phone as a social convenience and not just some hotline to be used only when disaster struck.

It was during the summer of 1969 that me and the band came to the inexorable realisation that this was serious; this was what they were going to do with their lives and although I didn't play an instrument, I was going to be a part of it. I have to say that they were starting to sound great. There was always a niggling thought in the back of my head that these were my mates and that was why I thought they were so good. But that summer I began to think, 'No, hang on a minute. They really are good. This stands up.' They were working hard at it, getting their chops together, still writing and rehearsing. For them it was really all about the writing. It's ironic that Genesis eventually became one of the most amazing and popular live bands, but actually in the early days we talked about the idea of performing behind a black curtain. Putting on a show was secondary. It was the music, the composition, the way of writing they developed. That was all that seemed to interest them in those days.

Ant and Mike loved doing 12-string acoustic guitar compositions with unusual tunings and many of the songs were based on ideas that flowed from that. There's a song on *Trespass* called 'Stagnation' that was written at the cottage, of which more later. It starts off purely acoustic with beautiful jangly guitars, then in come keyboards, then drums and bass. This was the pattern at that time, building from what Mike and Ant played on their acoustic instruments. It was kind of indie-folk if you like, not like traditional folk but something new that grew from folk-style guitar picking.

This led to one of the things that hampered them, tuning their guitars, because they needed to retune them between numbers. When you are playing at a college hop full of sweaty bodies and suddenly the temperature and the humidity go up, a cheap 12-string will go all over the place. Tuning two 12-string guitars used to take forever, which is how Peter came up with the creative solution of dressing up and talking to the audience. So began the madcap stories. Also we had really crap equipment that was always breaking down. Ant had his Vox AC30 but it was very much cobbled together. Tony Banks had a Hammond organ, not a B3 but a C3, the cheaper one, but we couldn't afford a proper Leslie so someone had made him one, a big square thing with a speaker and a vane in the top to make that distinctive swirly sound. I made the cover for it, sewn out of canvas. I remember doing it on Ant's mother's sewing machine at Send Barns and his dad coming in and saying, 'You'll make someone a lovely wife one day Richard.' In his world of merchant banking sewing was women's work.

Nevertheless, it was getting to the point where everyone was thinking, 'What are we going to do with this? What are we going to do now? How can we progress?' The Decca deal was dead. They had mixed feelings about the *From Genesis To Revelation* album, disappointed with the sound, disappointed with the mix. There were some good songs on it but they didn't like the quality of the production. Jonathan King had thrown them out of the studio, not willing to have any part of the mixing process. In a recent documentary King said he was someone who liked to be in charge of the creative process and to tell people what to do. This was not a band that was ever going to be told what to do by anyone. He said these guys were far too creative in their own right for a partnership with him to ever be a success. Also, King was a pop man, a singles man, very much into instant hits, while Genesis were moving to somewhere beyond pop, looking at the longer term, a way of doing things that was just beginning to emerge towards the end of the 60s.

Decca let them go without any hassle. They didn't make any money out of the album but they didn't care. In many ways they were fortunate in coming from families who were not just encouraging but also reasonably well off. Others weren't so lucky and might have had to struggle more. I don't think that Decca even paid an advance for the album because if there had been one, Genesis would have spent it on equipment. Advances weren't the norm then anyway. I think Ant's father got a solicitor to write to Decca and all was quickly sorted. It helped that they were all under 18.

The only thing I do remember about that album is that I bought a copy of *International Times*, the right-on leftie paper, and there was quite a favourable review in it. This was getting on towards the end of 1969. My immediate reaction was to dash into a callbox and ring Peter – I didn't want any boiling kettles to interrupt this call – and read it down the phone to him in Chobham. He was really chuffed that *IT* had given them a positive write-up.

As the summer of 1969 moved into autumn it became a sort of unspoken assumption that I was part of the group even though I wasn't one of the musicians. There was no one else involved, just me and the other five. I took on the roles of manager and roadie without actually being appointed. Lots of bands had a mate who drove them around and though I didn't actually get a licence until later that year, that was me.

By then, everything was converging. Mike was going to go to Farnham Tech, Peter to the London Film School and Tony back to Sussex University, but by now they all knew that more education was not a priority. In the meantime, they went through three drummers; as in *Spinal Tap*, drummers kept getting lost. Chris Stewart was replaced by John Silver who was replaced by John Mayhew, the latter found through an advert in *Melody Maker*. How else did anyone find musicians in those days?

I can't remember which one of the group suggested that what they really needed was somewhere they could go and live together like Traffic had done, in a cottage in the country. It was therefore strangely fortunate that one weekday while my parents were up in London, the cottage was burgled. The location was remote and my mother, who was nervous at the best of times, didn't feel comfortable going there anymore; they decided to sell it, but not until the following spring when the trees would be in full leaf and looking their best.

Naturally I thought, 'Hang on, it's ideal for the group' and asked my parents what they thought about the idea. 'My friends need a place to get together,' I told them. 'You're not going to sell the cottage until next spring. You don't want to go down there anymore.' In a strange way I think they suddenly saw that here was something for me to do, a role for their hopeless son. It was bizarre how they fought me tooth and nail about being a musician but didn't complain at all when I became a roadie, as if that were somehow more responsible, more mature than playing a guitar or singing. In their own way they found themselves able to support the choice that I wanted to make.

Genesis moved into Christmas Cottage near Wotton in October 1969. Not only did my parents offer them the cottage but my dad, who was still running the sales operation at Rank Hovis McDougall, bought an old LD delivery van from the company at cut price, got it painted and gave it to us. It was as if I was suddenly given total support for my new roles – a house, a van, the works.

Christmas Cottage was reached by a narrow winding lane next to a pub called The Wotton Hatch. The terrain was far from flat, with the lane dropping away alarmingly just as you approached the cottage. This always presented the old, overloaded van with a challenge. Not only that but there was no access to the cottage apart from the lane, so we couldn't park alongside and had to carry the gear up 24 steps hewn into the earth, then across the lawn and through the front door. On the plus side, it was isolated, surrounded by woodland, well off the beaten track. No one was likely to hear the group playing. No one was likely to disturb us. The cottage has been substantially altered since those days, extended on the ground floor, but it stands there still, hidden from the road and now approached by a winding drive to a parking area right beside the back door. Would that this drive had been available to us in those days!

At Christmas Cottage I was chief cook and bottle washer from October until the following April. Living there were Peter, Tony, Mike, Ant, John and me, all of us together in this three-bedroom cottage. What had been my parents' room had three mattresses on the floor for Ant, John and me. Mike had the little bedroom next to that and what had been my bedroom when I lived there with my parents, with its twin beds, was where Peter and Tony slept.

Tony recalls:

Sharing a room with Pete was fine. We always got on pretty well. I mean we'd fight and argue a bit but I remember that a lot of the cottage writing was quite stressful. Some of that concerned John Mayhew who wasn't… well, he was a good drummer but he was not creative. We were writing most of his parts to be honest and I remember him shouting at one point, when we were having an argument, 'You love humiliating me!' getting really uptight. It must have been hard for him. Here we were, four or five of us fresh out of public school with our own typical arcane public school language, and this guy comes in from the real world and has to put up with this behaviour. I did feel sorry for him but we were learning, we were really just beginning to learn how to be a band. I had the organ for the first time and didn't know what I was doing with it and we were trying to write songs. We were

*just starting off in that period and most of our songs had a sort
of normal structure and then they went wild for a bit and then
came back again.*

Not surprisingly with six young men under the same roof, it was
a real pressure cooker situation. It was winter, cold and damp, and
there were many times when you could cut the vibes in Peter and
Tony's room with a chainsaw. It was a very intense time, not least
because Peter was worried that his girlfriend Jill would leave him
for someone else. She was outgoing, very attractive, not one to sit
at home and mope while her man was away. Peter wasn't the only
guy interested in her.

Jill didn't have to worry about Peter though as we were very
insular at the cottage. We didn't even go to the local at the end of
the road. Genesis would never be your typical rock'n'rollers going
out, having a few beers. We didn't even have any booze in the
cottage. John and Mike used to enjoy a spliff of an evening, maybe
Ant too, but not Peter or Tony. In Mike's words:

I remember you giving me a spliff and listening to Procol Harum's
Salty Dog *on the headphones. As the cliché goes, my mind was
well and truly blown.*

John Mayhew, bless him, was a better carpenter than he was
a drummer. He made a wonderful back seat for the van so that we
could all travel together with room for the gear behind us. He put
together other bits and pieces too, like a cover for the organ and
badly needed stools for the stage. He was a fine guy, a good man to
have around, but he wasn't a good enough drummer for Genesis.

I found myself acting as a sort of soothing influence when
frustration got the better of the group. In his memoir, *The Living
Years*, Mike wrote:

*Someone would always be storming off upstairs or out the front
door and we'd have to regroup. Being a Libran I tended to be a
bit calmer but I think we would have killed each other without*

Rich – or starved. As well as being the peacemaker, Rich was our cook, which meant keeping us all fed on a virtually non-existent budget.

… If we hadn't had the cottage, we never would have got it together. Where would we have gone? There was no money. It gave us the chance to find out what we were about or could be about. Without Richard being there to make it flow, we would have bust up.

Their time was spent writing. The living room was set up with all the gear and to say they were industrious is an understatement. It was almost too disciplined. They would get up and have breakfast for a 10 o'clock start, with me watching and listening and making myself useful as best I could. I found it fascinating to witness how the whole process of creating songs came together. Mike would have a bit of a chord sequence, Tony had something to add and Peter had a rhythm that he often started a composition with (and still does to this day). He was a drummer, of course, and nowadays has numerous drum synthesisers but in those days he just had a bass drum to kick.

Ant was the musical giant. Something people always forget is that back then, he was far and away the most developed writer and the others followed him. The other crucial element was Tony's skill as a keyboard player and arranger. He was classically trained and like Guitar George in the Dire Straits song, he knew all the chords. Steve Hackett would later describe him as 'the chord king'. He knew a lot about harmony, how it functions within a song, and when someone would suggest going from this phrase to that one, he would think for a while, play his keyboard and figure out how to link them together. I was privileged to be in a position to watch this all happen before my eyes, witnessing the unfolding of what would become the album *Trespass*. There may have been some bits and pieces already in place before we moved to the cottage, but that's certainly where 'The Knife' and 'Stagnation' came in to being.

As Mike has said, I would cook the meals, drive, support them through emotional turmoil and do my best to fix any equipment when it went wrong. I was the support mechanism and as I watched the songs coming together I felt a glowing pride in what my friends were doing, a pride in being part of something that seemed to me to be genuinely worthy, something of merit.

Every now and then we'd have a weekend out and all go home. Ant, Mike and Peter would come back with great boxes full of groceries that their mums had bought. Money was very tight, maybe £30 here, £50 there from the odd gigs we did, amplified by the food parcels from our parents. Ant's mum would go through her freezer and one time sent him back with sweetbreads, otherwise known as calves' testicles, which I hadn't a clue how to cook. At the end of our stay in the cottage my parents were freaking out because they thought we'd have trashed it but they had taken most of their furniture out anyway, and I thought that by my standards, we'd kept it reasonably tidy. Then again, our standards rarely coincided.

All this time we were trying to get gigs and gain record company interest and perhaps also management. Because it was only an hour from the centre of London, Peter and I would get on the phone, cowering round the corner while the band was blasting away, and call up different labels and managers. Sometimes we'd even succeed in luring them down. These visits would include an introduction to the music and a roast chicken and homemade yoghurt, which I'd prepare earlier in the day. Lots of people said they would come and see us but strangely, their cars often broke down on the road from London to Dorking, a distance of only 30 miles. Two who did make it down to enjoy my culinary efforts (not to the mention the music) were Kenneth Pitt, who was David Bowie's manager at the time, and an agent called Markus Bicknell, who was to prove very helpful over the following few months.

Whenever we had a gig we had to hump the equipment up the steps to and from the cottage and in or out of the van, which was always a pain. The gigs were at various clubs in London, university and college hops, a whole string of them. We went to

Sunderland one night – in those days, it seemed like the end of the universe – where we supported Mott the Hoople who had just signed to Island. When we were on stage, Mott's singer, Ian Hunter, came and stood next to me at the mixing desk where I was doing the sound. All these fans were coming up to him and saying, 'What are you doing?' and he'd say, 'I'm watching Genesis.' In other words, 'Fuck off I'm listening,' which I interpreted as a compliment.

Mike recalls that tour:

> I remember feeling that the cottage was like a cocoon, but we left the cocoon in mid-December to go on a mini tour of the north, gigs in Birmingham and Manchester. It was exciting but scary. In Birmingham we played in a social club and afterwards slept on the floor in the changing rooms. For some inexplicable reason, in the middle of the night the under-floor heating came on. It was so hot we couldn't walk on the floor. We had to throw shirts down and use them as stepping stones.

Our next big break was at Friars music club in Aylesbury, which turned out to be very important for the band's evolution. After Sunderland, Mott played there and Ian told Dave Stopps, the resident promoter, how good we were. So I rang Stopps and said, 'I'm Richard Macphail from Genesis.' I got just the response I was hoping for: 'Oh yeah, Mott the Hoople told me about you. Do you want to come and play at Friars?' So we did. This turned out to be the first of many happy gigs there.

Another rich seam for Genesis was the college circuit. On one occasion, an agent set up a showcase for likely groups at the Queen Elizabeth College in Campden Hill Road off Kensington High Street. There were about a dozen bands including us, and we each did a 20-minute showcase for invited bookers from various colleges. For some reason, John Anthony, the record producer, was there. He was the in-house producer and occasional A&R man at Charisma Records, before which he had been involved with Trident Studios in St Anne's Court between

Dean and Wardour Street. Evidently he was impressed as he told Tony Stratton-Smith, the boss of Charisma, about us.

Also at that time, we did a gig in Canterbury with a group called Rare Bird who were already signed to Charisma. It turned into a mutual love-fest with Rare Bird really liking us and vice versa. Graham Stansfield, their keyboard player, evidently went into the Charisma offices on Dean Street the next day and said, 'This band is amazing, you must sign them.'

As it happened, our booking agent, Markus Bicknell, had just got us a Monday night residency in the room above Ronnie Scott's, the legendary jazz club in Soho. The management at Ronnie's were desperately envious of the success of the Marquee Club around the corner so they had opened Upstairs at Ronnie's as a bit of added competition. We somehow got in there just as it was beginning. Once again, we had to lug the gear up countless stairs and guess what? Nobody came. However, one fateful Monday night, Tony Stratton-Smith, his second in command Gail Colson, her brother Glen and John Anthony came and listened to our set.

Tony, known to one and all as Strat, was a jovial, avuncular fellow, very well-spoken, on the portly side, fond of his drink, well travelled and worldly wise, but he wasn't one for going and seeing bands much. In fact, the only reason he would ever leave London was for a race meeting at Plumpton or Epsom; but because all he needed to do was walk down the street and around the corner to Ronnie's to see Genesis, he came, and he liked what he saw.

And that was that.

Chapter 7

A LITTLE BIT OF CHARISMA

*Leaving the cottage was like being launched on a voyage
in a leaky boat with only half an oar, sailing away
on some sort of mad adventure, the six of us
with no compass and just the stars and
a few songs to navigate by.*

One thing that can't have impressed the Charisma people was the size of the audience we attracted to Upstairs at Ronnie's. Ronnie Scott used to joke that if someone rang the club on a quiet night to ask what time the show started, he'd ask, 'What time can you get here?' It's quite likely that Strat and his team were the only ones there to watch Genesis that night in March 1970. I remember another night when the audience consisted only of Peter's girlfriend Jill, a pal of mine called David Vaughan-Thomas, the son of the broadcaster Wynford Vaughan-Thomas, and, of all people, Chris Langham, the brilliant comedy writer and actor who was later sent to jail for possessing child pornography. Genesis always did attract an eclectic crowd.

There were never more than ten people present but that didn't deter Charisma. Gail Colson, Strat's PA, asked Peter for his phone number after the set and got in touch with him the next day to arrange a meeting at their offices in Dean Street. She didn't hang around. Peter, Mike, Tony, Ant and John all attended and Strat offered them the whole dream package: a record deal, management and even a booking agency. Charisma were in cahoots with an agent called Terry King who started booking their gigs from then on. Ant's father provided a solicitor and they all signed on the dotted line.

The first order of business was to record another album, in reality their second. Most people probably look on *Trespass* as their debut since the *Genesis To Revelation* LP recorded for Decca was a bit of a false start. So without delay they went into Trident Studios in St Anne's Court and began recording the songs they had been writing at Christmas Cottage. John Anthony took on the important role of producer.

In the meantime we'd all moved out of the cottage and were living all over the place. Quoting Mike again:

After the cottage we became something proper. It gave us a springboard. We were still not fully formed but we had a reason to be a band.

Peter got a flat in Wandsworth where he lived with Jill. Tony went to live with a friend in Earls Court where he met Margaret McBain whom he later married. John found a flat in Colville Terrace, Notting Hill, a very groovy area then and still is. Ant stayed in Send and Mike, who now had a beautiful girlfriend called Josie, stayed at Farnham. I got a ground floor room in a house in Cavendish Road, Kilburn that I shared with Gerard Selby who came on board for a while as our second roadie. Gerard was a childhood friend of Miranda Davies, one of my Millfield buddies. He was a good strong lad from a farming family from Devon and at a loose end, so it seemed natural for us to become the Genesis road crew.

At the Kilburn house there was a communal bathroom, two shillings in the slot for a bath. Another friend from Millfield, Jimmy Western and his unbelievably gorgeous and voracious girlfriend Jenny lived in the attic. Jimmy satisfied Jenny on many levels but physically – you might call it an open relationship. Jimmy would go off to work and when I could, I'd pop upstairs… Jimmy will have known what was going on because later that summer, we enjoyed a threesome in a tent at the first Glastonbury Festival.

Leaving the cottage was like being launched on a voyage in a leaky boat with only half an oar, sailing away on some sort of mad adventure, the six of us with no compass and just the stars and a few songs to navigate by. It was very delicate. We could have sunk. Somehow Strat, this great admiral-like man with a huge friendly smile, came along and swept us up into his arms and we became part of his fleet. Miraculously, everything was now taken care of.

My parents sold the cottage but it's still there, a nostalgic reminder of a time when Genesis lived hand-to-mouth, all crammed together. I've been back a few times, most recently in September of 2016 with Chris Charlesworth, my co-author of these memoirs.

Years after we left I remember my mother had a conversation with Mrs Rutherford. My mum still thought that all I did was drive the band around, but Mike's mum knew better and told her I had a key position in the group, that I was an important piece of the framework that held it all together. She put my mum straight about all the many roles that I filled. For the first time she realised I was more than just an unskilled labourer.

There are some fans who still believe that Peter usurped my position as the singer in the group. My deeply held conviction is that this was exactly how it was meant to be. Back at the cottage I'd be in the kitchen peeling potatoes and cooking sausages. I'd hear them practising and writing, a few scraps of this and that and somehow out of this process, a little bit of magic would emerge. I knew as clear as day that I couldn't do that. I knew what I could do but it wasn't what Peter, Mike, Tony and Ant were creating. I also knew that there was lots of stuff that I could do that they couldn't. They needed me like Bertie Wooster needed Jeeves and it was obvious where the roles lay. They had their heads in the music, thinking about the next chord sequence, how to jump into the next verse. I knew they had to eat and where they needed to go and how to get them there. Not once was I ever envious that Peter was the singer and I was peeling the potatoes.

There was a second meeting with Charisma that I did attend, to sort out all the practicalities like transport and what we were going to live on. Strat suggested that everyone should be given a living allowance of £15 a week. 'That would be suitable,' he declared in his fruity voice. At which point John Mayhew chirped up and said, 'I think we could manage on £10,' and everybody glared at him and kicked him under the table. Because of him we ended up on a tenner, the same for all of us, including me. It wasn't that we needed much money really. All we needed was to be able to pay our rent and eat. The money was paid in cash that I'd collect from Charisma each week and dish out in £1 notes to each member of the band.

At this point, none of the band members had a reliable car to get to and from our growing number of gigs. It just so happened that Peter's mother Irene had recently been thinking about giving up smoking. Peter's sister, Anne Goldsworthy, remembers:

> *Mum was very keen to get Peter a new car. Dad thought it was a bit too indulgent. Mum told Dad that she would give up smoking if Peter got his car. A discussion took place where Mum said how much the car would cost. There was a short pause while Dad's engineer's brain worked out the payback period and he said, 'We'll get our money back in a little over a year – OK, let's do it.' Thus Peter acquired a shiny, new Hillman Imp that became the band's mode of transport.*

The next thing for me was to sort out getting a new van. We had to retire the old one to the scrapheap, waving goodbye with a tear in our eyes to the faithful bread van that Dad had bought for us. Charisma used to source their bands' vans from a guy called Reg King, a sort of all-round Mr Fix It for the music business, a bit of a hard man too. Someone told me he used to be Keith Richards's driver, which I guess meant bodyguard. He was very flamboyant with dyed blond hair and a lot of bling before we called it that –

big rings on his fingers and a thick chain around his neck. A bit frightening. I was sent by Gail to see him at his office in Carlisle Street, coincidentally in the same building where Jonathan King had had his offices.

'Reg'll fix you up with a van,' Gail told me, so off I went around the corner from Dean Street but, when I got there, well… there were splodges of fresh blood on the stairs. It turned out Reg had just nutted somebody. Seeing my alarm, he got on the phone to Gail. 'Richard's round 'ere,' he explained. 'He saw the claret on the stairs and he's in a bit of a state of shock. I'll sort him out.'

It didn't take me long to realise that this kind of thing was a daily occurrence in Reg's life. He was a tough guy but he adored me. I don't think he'd ever met a public school boy before and we got on like a house on a fire, in spite of what might have seemed like chalk and cheese. Goodness knows what that day's altercation was about – probably that he was owed money that wasn't forthcoming. Ever present was Reg's sidekick Paddy, an incredibly dour accountant character; he never said a word, just glared at everyone.

Reg himself drove a 1968 Sedan de Ville open-top Cadillac, but he provided Ford Transits for the bands. He had a seemingly endless fleet of vehicles held together with brown paper and string. Reg soon found us a long wheelbase transit with windows. You could see all the gear inside but somehow none of it was ever nicked. Maybe London's van thieves recognised one of Reg's vans and steered clear of them to avoid any more claret being spilt on the stairs.

Next on the agenda was a much needed equipment upgrade. We went off to WEM (Watkins Electric Music) in Stockwell to visit their factory and got ourselves a PA system and Mike upgraded to a decent bass amp. I remember that we set up all this new gear in a village hall somewhere between Send and Woking to try it out. I got it going and… Wow! The band had never sounded so good. The difference with a decent PA was astounding. You could actually hear Peter singing. A revelation. After we'd moved the gear out of the cottage we simply stored it in the van wherever it was parked, or at the studio in Soho where they were recording. I'd simply deliver it to wherever it was needed.

Since Charisma had come up with the whole package, Terry King began to get us gigs right away; he and Paul Conroy and Chris Briggs, two bookers who worked for him, both of whom would go on to have stellar careers in the music business. Charisma had an operations manager called Fred Munt whose job was to oversee the day-to-day activities of the bands on the label: Rare Bird, Van Der Graaf Generator and The Nice, though the latter soon split up when Keith Emerson formed ELP. Fred had worked for the Bonzo Dog Doodah Band and was immortalised in their song 'Intro and Outro' as the 'Wild Man Of Borneo', on bongos of course. I can remember helping him to pour Bonzo's Viv Stanshall into a taxi many times after he had quaffed too many sherbets at the Chasse, the poky private members bar for music biz types on Wardour Street where we used to go for drinks after the office had closed.

I owe a lot to Fred. He taught me all there was to being a roadie, big things and small, tips of the trade that help to ease you through this most arduous of jobs. I remember in New York, Fred and I rented a car and he told me that whenever you were given the rental documents the first thing to do was to put them in the glove compartment. Otherwise you might lose them. It might sound obvious but to this day I always do it and I've never once lost my rental car documents. Every time I perform this simple action I think of Fred Munt. Eventually Fred married Gail Colson but, sadly, it didn't last.

It took Genesis a couple of months to make *Trespass* but I have to say that, personally, I was hugely disappointed when I heard it. I used to blame John Anthony but that's not really fair, as I don't think he was the right producer for them. To be honest I'm not sure that anyone would have been. I just knew what they sounded like live because by this point I was mixing the sound on stage and knew that sound hadn't made it on to the recording. People who had never heard the band live loved *Trespass* and it's got some great music on it but for me it lacked the power that I knew they had, the power that came over when they were playing live on stage.

The album was due to be released in the autumn and lots of gigs were coming up, including the early ones at Friars, but another problem was looming, a massive complication known only to the inner circle. Ant had developed acute stage fright and was really struggling with it. He talked about having had an out of body experience on stage; it was that bad. One time we played a college in Hackney with an audience of around 25 people but he was terrified out of his mind, so much so that he developed glandular fever. The stage fright was making him ill and affecting his ability to play as well as he was capable of. Ant didn't have an actual breakdown but he was close to it. He told Peter he just couldn't go on and Peter called a band meeting to tell us the news.

The meeting took place one night after we'd played at the Marquee, in the van at the back of the club where we parked to load in the gear. We'd done our set and when the other band came on Peter ominously told us that we had to go and sit in the van and have a talk. That's when he announced that Ant was leaving. Of course I knew Ant was struggling but *Trespass* wouldn't have been anything like the album it was without him. So there we were again – Peter, Tony, Mike and me, significantly without John Mayhew. Everyone was in shock. What were we going to do? The three of them actually proposed giving up. They thought they couldn't go on without Ant but I wasn't having it: 'For God's sake, we've come this far, you can't give up now. It's too good. You have to go on.'

Tony remembers it well:

When Ant left I thought, 'That's going to be it.' I thought that because Ant was Richard's closest friend in the group he would go too. Obviously we were very dependent on Richard. I thought that Ant was the most dominant person in the group, the leader in a way. He was the one that propelled us forward as writers. Mike followed Ant, Peter and I were much less sure of ourselves. So I thought that's probably it. I remember a conversation with Peter and Mike during which Richard insisted, 'You really must keep going.' I thought that if he was saying that, as Ant's friend, that made a big difference to me. Peter and Mike... we weren't sure and we talked together, and then decided, 'Yes, let's find a replacement.' We knew how difficult that would be but we did it.

I like to think that I persuaded them not to give up that night but it was Tony, the voice of reason, whose argument carried the day. He was the last one to speak. 'All right,' he said. 'We'll go on but we have to get a new drummer.'

Tony recalls this crucial decision as if it happened yesterday:

We had to get a good drummer and I think we all agreed with that. That was a very important thing to me because I felt that we needed a drummer who was creative and someone who didn't have to be told what to do. In fact, finding a drummer turned out to be a lot easier than finding a guitarist.

Many years later, in an acceptance speech when he won a Prog Rock God Award in 2015, Tony mentioned this, saying that without my encouragement they might well not have gone on after Ant's departure. He never actually said this to me personally but suddenly there we were at an important awards ceremony and he remembered that incident after all that had passed between us.

I think we all knew deep down that John Mayhew wasn't up to it but only Tony was prepared to say it out loud. Tony is a very smart guy and he saw past the problem with Ant and realised it was an opportunity to get a better drummer. If they were going to make one change they might as well make two and he was quite right. So the decision was made. We climbed out of the van and went back into the club, me to get the gear to load up, Peter, Mike and Tony to give John Mayhew the news. The problems were solved or so we hoped.

A day or two later, we told the people at Charisma that Ant was leaving the band and we were also going to get another drummer. They were worried but mightily relieved that we weren't going to split up. *Trespass* had been recorded and was about to come out, and they wouldn't have wanted to release an album by a non-existent band. I don't know how much we owed them by then – a few thousand quid maybe as they'd picked up the studio costs and paid our wages. It was all an advance against future royalties. I do remember we were in the hole to the tune of £300,000 by the time *Foxtrot*, the third Charisma album, was released.

To find a new guitarist and drummer we put another advert into the classified pages of *Melody Maker* and among those who saw it was a guy named Phil Collins, then playing with a group called Flaming Youth. I think it impressed everyone that he was actually a professional musician earning his living as a drummer, though his band's career had come to an abrupt halt with the failure of the album *Ark 2*, created by the song writing duo Ken Howard and Alan Blakely. Despite a lot of hype it had fallen on deaf ears. Phil's departure effectively sank the Ark and the group with it.

Auditions for drummers were held at Peter's parents' farm, Deep Pool in Chobham. It was a glorious summer's day in August, warm and sunny and although Phil was third on the list of six and not due to play until 11, he was there at nine in the morning, keen as mustard, an early clue as to his character. He was asked to sit and wait by the swimming pool and because the windows of the house were open, was able to listen to the two drummers before him. Being the extremely musical guy that he is, he instantly absorbed everything he heard.

Finally it was Phil's turn. He set up his kit, left-handed we noticed, which proved annoying in the future as no one else could ever get behind his drums and have a go. But he just sat down and played, no messing, no questions. It was a revelation. It was as if he'd learned the songs already – which he hadn't, he'd just heard them through the window – and he did it his way. It was astonishing.

Tony recalls:

Although at the audition Phil was definitely the best – Peter and I were convinced of that – Mike didn't seem totally sold. Two of the other guys were quite good, I remember. If Phil hadn't been

there we would have used one of them. However, we liked Phil
for all sorts of reasons. He just made everything sound good.

They did hear out the others but there was no question that Phil was the man. He was living in Hounslow, at home with his family, and it turned out that he already knew Strat from the Chasse, the Soho drinking club, and the Marquee where he'd done casual work sweeping the floor and clearing away the chairs.

We set up a rehearsal at the semi-derelict Maltings building in Farnham, an old brewery now home to a large flock of pigeons, down the road from Mike's house. It was arranged that Mike would show Phil the songs before Tony and Peter came in. I was there to handle the gear. More so than at the audition, for me this was another musical eye-opener as I had never realised what a difference a drummer could make. I always thought the drummer was not much more than a human metronome at the back but, oh boy, Phil transformed the way things sounded to an unbelievable degree.

Tony agrees:

Not being the greatest timekeeper myself, it was just great to be
able to play the thing and see that it worked. Phil was doing it.
He kept it going.

In his 2016 autobiography, *Not Dead Yet*, a rather dour title that I certainly wouldn't have chosen myself, Phil writes of his introduction to the Genesis gang:

A constant presence is Richard Macphail. He'd been the singer
in Anon, one of the pre-Genesis bands at Charterhouse. He's
the road manager and sound engineer, and a big spliff head.
Maybe he has to be, as he sleeps in The Maltings, sharing a berth
with the pigeons and their guano and guarding the gear. He
introduces me to the pleasure of the stoned headphone listening
experience. Crosby, Stills, Nash and Young's Déjà Vu is not
long out, and Richard brings round the LP, builds a giant joint

*and instructs Mike and me to immerse ourselves in the sonic
majesties of 'Carry On'. It's not quite kicking open the doors of
perception, but I am knocking gently.'*

Reading this now, I can agree with Phil's memories but, in my
own defence, I am bound to say that I never got stoned *before*
going to work. It was only a recreational thing.

Phil and I got on like a house on fire and we've remained
friends to this day. He wasn't an uptight public schoolboy who
had trouble expressing his feelings. He spoke as he saw. He was
always upbeat too – funny, enthusiastic, like a puppy dog with his
tongue hanging out, always straining on the leash, raring to go.
He was a joy to be around and very down to earth. The force of
his personality transformed the band in every way because of his
delightful honesty. All of this business of people getting up and
storming out was completely alien to him. If anyone did that, Phil
would look up and go, 'What happened?' with this expression of
bewilderment on his face. That was simply not his way of doing
things. You got it off your chest right away, out in the open and
didn't allow anything to fester until it simply got worse.

Phil's way of thinking really did prick any lingering pomposity
within the group. It was an astonishing transformation and very
fortunate that he arrived when he did because our problems
weren't over.

At gigs Mike would play rhythm guitar and bass pedals since,
unusually, Genesis had no designated bass player. However, we
still desperately needed a replacement guitarist. We tried Phil's
friend, Ronnie Caryl, the guitarist from Flaming Youth, but he
didn't work out, so we bought a Hohner electric piano for Tony
and plugged it into Ant's amp. This way, Tony would play the
guitar solos with his right hand while he was playing the organ
chords with his left.

That's how, when *Trespass* came out, we fulfilled the gigs as
a four piece, which is probably when I ruined my hearing. We had
this wonderful WEM PA with a mixing desk but we couldn't afford
a multicore lead from the amps to the desk, so I wasn't able to mix

the sound from the back of the audience. I would sit directly in front of the speakers, which totally blasted my ears. I would fall asleep every night with jungle noises ringing in my head.

We carried on as a four piece for two or three months with Mike shouldering many of the guitar duties until Steve Hackett answered the ad in *Melody Maker* and joined Genesis towards the end of the year. He, too, did an audition like Phil, though it was more of a job interview in his case. He was, as he later referred to himself, a legend in his own bedroom that happened to be in a block of flats in Victoria. The balance in the group was tipping away from the public school end towards guys with more regular backgrounds. Straight away it was clear that Steve was interested in all the things that Genesis were into: acoustic guitars, different tunings and complex arrangements. He was clearly not interested in being a guitar hero. He simply wanted to play well without drawing attention to himself, always a team player.

One day in early December I left the Charisma office and drove along Old Compton Street towards Charing Cross Road when a police car suddenly overtook me and jammed right in front of us demanding that we pull over. A rotund plain-clothes police officer jumped out, came running back and told me to get out of the van. 'Where are you going,' he screamed. 'What have you got in the back of the van?' I opened up the back and a pickaxe handle fell out. I had found it lying around in the back yard of a college where we'd done a gig, shoved it into the back of the van in case it came in useful one day and forgot about it. When the policeman asked what it was for I mumbled something incoherent. 'It's an offensive weapon,' he said. 'It's only a pickaxe handle,' I replied. At that moment a uniformed officer got out of the police car and shouted back to him. 'Sergeant Long [that was his name], this isn't the van we're looking for. It's in Tottenham Court Road.' The Sergeant exercised his authority by telling me to get rid of it, then rushed back into his car which zoomed off with lights flashing and siren howling up Charing Cross Road. I never gave it another thought. But I should have done.

A couple of weeks later, just before Christmas, Charisma was throwing a lunch-time party at the Marquee. Gail had asked me to come to the office because she wanted a lift with the cake, so at about 11.30 a.m. I showed up at the office and we loaded it into the van. There we were, with me in the driving seat, Gail in the passenger seat and the cake between us. We set off down Brewer Street and had only been going for about two minutes when yet another police car came screaming past and pulled us over. You've guessed it: it was the fearsome Sergeant Long. He walked straight up to the cab.

'Have you got rid of it?'
'No.' I said.
'Right, you're nicked. I warned you. You're in possession of an offensive weapon.'

I was taken to Bow Street, leaving Gail stranded in the van. She had to find someone else to drive her over to the Marquee to deliver the cake while I was arrested and charged. I was told later that Strat rang up Bow Street Police Station and tried to speak to the most senior officer. 'He's an Admiral's son,' he told whoever was on the other end of the line. 'You must release him immediately.' I don't know whether he really thought that or simply said it because he thought it might get me released. Maybe he was mixing me up with Mike's dad who was a Navy man. After a couple of hours I was bailed in time to get to the Marquee and enjoy the party.

A few weeks later I was up in court, an experience that brought home to me what being part of the Charisma family was all about. Strat or Gail had arranged for Dennis Muirhead, a lawyer famous for defending people arrested for drugs, to act for me. There I was in the court room and there was Sergeant Long with his notebook, reciting how he'd apprehended me with a pickaxe handle on my person. In the end, the case was thrown out of court because a pickaxe handle is not, *per se*, an offensive weapon and they had no evidence that I had used it or intended to use it as such. If it had been a knuckleduster or a cosh it would have been different, so they had to let me off. The only addendum to this story is that years later, when Genesis played at Knebworth, I was backstage in the bar and ran into Dennis Muirhead. I was then able to thank him belatedly for getting me off, which meant I didn't have a police record. I am forever grateful to him for that.

Meanwhile, Steve Hackett was settling into Genesis, though his initiation was not without its dilemmas. In his own words:

The first gig was at University College in Gower Street. For me it was a disaster. Up to then I'd been using a borrowed fuzzbox, a real semi-pro thing, or using Tony's Marshall Superfuzz, so everything worked fine on that and I remembered the tunes on it but on the night in question you gave me a Shaftesbury Duo Fuzz which is a great fuzzbox. You couldn't get a Marshall Superfuzz and I thought, 'Oh, this sounds nice,' and when we did the sound check it seemed fine, but of course by the time everyone was playing, it was much louder and things started to feed back endlessly and so it really put me off and I forgot everything I'd learned about this music. I remember a blazing row after the show and I was thinking it was all my fault. In hindsight, it wasn't anything to do with me. That was my most embarrassing moment on stage, being on stage with highly arranged music and with the total inability to remember a note because I couldn't control my sound. Not a good start. I thought, 'That's it, I've blown it.'

Things looked up for Steve at his second Genesis gig, at a teacher training college in Bangor, North Wales:

We played in a classroom to about three people sitting at their desks. This was exactly what I needed, to have the pressure taken off, a paid rehearsal in front of people. So I got through that... extreme relief. We were doing the Lyceum the following day. I was still living at home and my mother exclaimed to me on the day, 'Oh my darling, you're GREEN!' My face was literally green with nerves because that was the biggest gig you could do in England at that time. The Lyceum was it. And I thought, 'I'd better not blow this.'

Genesis did the Lyceum gig that December but again, it was a bit nerve-wracking for Steve as he didn't have any gigging experience. At the end of their set the others all just sort of melted away and walked off stage like they usually did but Steve didn't know what to do. He stood there thinking, 'Well, what happens now? We've played the songs, now what?' I saw him looking lost, and took him by the hand and led him off stage. 'I remember you came on stage and said to me, "The gig's over",' Steve has told me. '"You can leave now." I felt a little bit like a shell-shock victim.'

Like Phil he was perfect for Genesis, exactly the right musician with a superb technique and a personality that fitted in with the band.

So now they were five again, the classic line-up. Full steam ahead.

MY BOOK OF GENESIS

Chapter 8

MELLOTRONICS

When we played at the Nottingham Boat House,
the promoter cut a huge piece of the stair rail off
with a chainsaw so that we could get the
Mellotron up the stairs.

Like all bands of their stature, Genesis gigged continually in those days, not tours as such, just endless dates that would have been set up by Terry King's agency and relayed to Fred Munt at Charisma. I, in my turn, would call in to the office to receive my week's itinerary. Genesis were hardworking and the gigs served two purposes: exposing them to potential fans and developing their stagecraft, all the while making them a better band.

The gigs could be anywhere. There was no especially logical progression that made any geographical sense and because we couldn't afford hotels, we would always drive back to London afterwards and then head off to somewhere else the next day. It was nuts really, often getting back at two in the morning and setting off seven or eight hours later. When he was writing his book, Phil sent me an email: 'We fucking worked hard, didn't we?' Dead right. We did work hard, easily playing five or six gigs a week.

At this time we were paid around £50 or £75 a night and it was my responsibility to collect the money from the promoter after the show. I got one of those helpful clicker devices because quite often we were on a split of the door and I would click around the audience to make sure it was the same size as the promoter claimed. Heaven forbid that a rock promoter would fiddle the numbers, like lopping 50 or so off the top, but it was wise to check all the same.

As well as the van with the equipment that I drove, Peter had the Hillman Imp, a really small car with only room for four people in comfort. Three of them, Mike, Steve and Tony, would go with Peter and Phil would usually come with Gerard and me in the van. We'd need to go early to get loaded in and set up. It was fine by me that Phil came with us because it meant he could set up his own kit, which was one less thing for us to do. He was always so very keen; he couldn't wait to get started.

Another reason Phil liked to travel with us was because I had a cassette player in the van, a phenomenon that was fairly unusual at the time. It wasn't actually installed, it just sat on the dashboard with speakers on either side; it's a miracle it was never stolen. More often than not Phil would bring novel mix tapes he had made. He was into all sorts of music that I'd never heard of. He turned me on to American drummers like Billy Cobham, who was with John's McLaughlin's Mahavishnu Orchestra, and Bernard Purdie, the Atlantic session man who played on Aretha Franklin records. Who can forget his astonishing contribution to 'Young, Gifted and Black'? Phil was into Yes as well, in fact, he nearly joined them at one point. The singer, Jon Anderson, had his eye on Phil and I found out much later that he wasn't the only one trying to poach him. They'd hear us playing and think, 'Bloody hell, he's a good drummer.' Phil and Yes's drummer Bill Bruford were great friends and when, much later, Peter left Genesis and Phil became the front man, Bill was the drummer they brought in at Phil's request.

At the weekends it was usually college gigs while during the week we played lots of little clubs like Farx in Southall, just west of Ealing, or the Half Moon in Putney, often either in the back room of a pub or above one. Although *Trespass* didn't exactly set the world alight, we could see that the audiences were gradually growing. We'd go to one of these small clubs, returning a few months later and invariably there'd be a few more people.

These audiences, small as they were, always knew what to expect with Genesis. They knew they weren't going to be bopping to rock'n'roll or R&B because the music Genesis performed veered unexpectedly from fast to slow, loud to soft – what the music papers were beginning to call 'progressive rock'. The initiated crowd would sit on the floor and listen. This was the height of the post-hippy era with men in greatcoats or their mum's fur coat with the sleeves cut off, tie-dyed t-shirts and loon pants or big flared jeans with darts in the leg to maximise the flare. Often boys and girls alike had the same length of hair, parted in the centre, and the girls would have sewn patches on to their boyfriends' jeans. Neil Young featured his jean patches on the back of the cover of his *After the Gold Rush* album. Cat Stevens wrote a song called 'Oh Very Young' about having to finally let go of his patches or perhaps the loss of the innocence of youth. 'And the patches make the goodbye harder still.'

Towards the end of 1970 or the beginning of 1971 we acquired a Mellotron, a keyboard that triggered the playback of a pre-recorded sound. We bought it from King Crimson because we loved their sound, especially the way they used their Mellotron on *In the Court Of the Crimson King*, an album that was very influential for Genesis. Gail contacted David Enthoven and Johnny Gaydon of EG Management, who managed King Crimson, and their guitarist, Robert Fripp, came to the office to talk to us about the sound made possible for them by the Mellotron. It turned out that the instrument they had used on that album had been damaged in a fire, but only the case, which someone had painted over in black. Having acquired a shiny new one, they were more than happy to let Genesis buy the old one from them.

It wouldn't be unreasonable to assume that Tony Banks was the inspiration behind acquiring a Mellotron but at the outset it was new boy Steve Hackett, a huge King Crimson fan, who urged the others into getting one:

I wanted Genesis to be an orchestra. I was desperate to get a Mellotron. I was working on them like Chinese water torture for six months. Eventually, I went down with Tony to meet Crimson when they were rehearsing in a dingy cellar off the Fulham Palace Road and met Robert [Fripp] for the first time.

The Mellotron was never designed for rock music, more for use in pubs where someone could play it and simulate a whole orchestra. Nor was it meant to be carted around as it was the original double keyboard instrument and really heavy. Gerard and I were strong enough – the two of us could shift a Hammond organ – but we couldn't move this beast with less than four people. It was an absolute monster, never meant for going on the road.

The Mellotron altered the sound of the band, moving it dramatically forward. As Steve says:

Straightaway Tony started mixing the brass with the strings and began heading towards the sound that was to become 'Watcher Of the Skies.' That was one of the things that transformed the band. The other thing was Peter being prepared to dress up as virtually anything and suddenly you had pictures of us on the front of Melody Maker. He did crazy things with his hair, with his clothes and there was nothing he wouldn't do on stage. The rest of us were just getting on with making the music. Another realisation was, 'Look, we've got to get our own light show.' We were not content with those strobes that everyone remembers, and all those oily bubbles that tended to make the bands look mucky. It was growing... we had someone out front mixing sound; we had someone working lights. If you're doing this sort of music you have to be able to sound like an orchestra, a choir, a rock band, a pop group, you name it and we were doing it. You need all that going for it because if you don't people aren't going to be able to follow the complexity of the music. It'll be pulling in too many different directions.

All of this additional baggage meant we needed a bigger van. Back we went to Reg King who got us a box transit, a Luton van, which was always hopelessly overloaded and under-powered. It didn't have any stream lining, just a vertical wall behind the cab, and it was incredibly slow. We'd be grinding uphill on a motorway at forty miles per hour with huge trucks flying past us. Not that there were many motorways in those days. The M1 went as far as Watford Gap and then fizzled out and if you were going up to Manchester or Liverpool, the M6 picked up again way north of Birmingham. We would have to do this horrible Cannock Chase run around Birmingham. For gigs in the West Country we'd go so far along the M4 but once it stopped, we'd have to take A-roads and go through towns as there weren't many city bypass roads either. It's hard to imagine now in these days of a full motorway network. Phil's cassette tapes made many a journey infinitely more tolerable for the three of us.

Because Genesis were working so hard the only other bands we ever saw were those who played on the same bill as us, and only then if Genesis bothered to stick around. We always used to be on first, bottom of the bill, and since the band usually wanted to get home as quickly as possible they'd all pile into the Hillman Imp, including Phil. I would see other bands while I was packing up the gear backstage, winding up all the cables and trying not to forget things. We'd get there in the late afternoon and it would take a couple of hours to set up. This all depended on the 'get in', i.e. how easy it was to unload everything from the van and carry it onto the stage. Rooms above a pub, with narrow flights of stairs to negotiate, were the worst. When we played at the Nottingham Boat House, the promoter had to cut a huge piece of the stair rail off with a chainsaw so that we could get the Mellotron up the stairs. Sometimes the band got a sound check before they went on and other times they didn't, all depending on the attitude of the artists who were topping the bill. You were totally at the mercy of the main band, some of whom were less generous than others in this respect.

We played with so many bands, too many to remember, but Barclay James Harvest and Caravan were a couple where the promoter seemed to have made an attempt to present groups likely to attract fans with similar musical tastes. Often, though, we were completely mismatched. At some clubs we played on our own and sometimes a local act would go on first, often some guy with an acoustic guitar singing his own songs, a would-be Cat Stevens or James Taylor. The stages were almost always tiny, no more than a little triangle in the corner of the room, but the college gigs were better, though at these there was more chance of a mismatch.

One of the colleges we played around this time was Ewell Tech near Epsom in Surrey where the social secretaries had been Paul Conroy and Chris Briggs, both of whom would work for Charisma and make it big in the music business, Conroy as CEO at various major labels and Briggs in A&R. Nevertheless they booked us for a gig with The Keef Hartley Band, far from an ideal match as Hartley, who'd made his name as drummer for John Mayall, specialised in blues rock. Also on the same bill was an early line-up of Queen, in those days a cross between David Bowie and Led Zeppelin, another bad match for Genesis. We went on first but Freddie Mercury wasn't the Freddie Mercury that everyone remembers now. He was singing but just sitting down playing keyboards, not prancing about waving half a mic stand like a sergeant major's baton. What I remember most about that night was Brian May, an amazing guitarist. There was a story going around later that Peter tried to poach Queen's drummer, Roger Taylor, for Genesis but I don't think it's true as by this time we already had Phil. Then again, I've heard it the other way around, that Queen tried to poach Phil, a drum swop. Singing drummers were evidently at a premium in those days.

Years later, at the last concert Genesis ever played in London [July 8th 2007 at Twickenham], I was talking to Brian May who'd been a fan of Genesis ever since that night at Ewell Tech. I asked him if he remembered that occasion, and he replied: 'Yes, that was the night we met our bass player John Deacon.'

Meanwhile, the prospects for Genesis were slowly but surely getting better. We had our first £100 gig, at Newbury, and our first trip abroad, in March 1971, to Belgium. Most fans assume that Italy was the first foreign territory to take Genesis to their hearts but actually we broke first in Belgium, then Italy a year later, in 1972. No one seems to know now how or why Belgium came first. I would go into the office and Fred Munt would have the diary of gigs that had been booked by Terry King, and he'd say, 'Right Rich, you've got Sunderland tomorrow or Leeds or Coventry or whatever.' And one day he said, 'Right Rich, you're off to Belgium in two weeks.'

The big deal as far as I was concerned was dealing with the *carnet*, a right old headache for roadies everywhere. I had to make this exhaustive list of everything, all the gear that was in the van, and take it to the Chamber of Commerce, put up a hefty bond and tell them where we were going. You needed one piece of paper for leaving one country and another for going into the next, and it all had to be 100% correct, otherwise you ran the risk of losing your bond.

We crossed the Channel, taking a ferry from Dover to Ostend. It was the middle of winter and there was hardly anyone else on board. By this time Peter's Hillman Imp had been retired and Reg had provided us with yet another van, a small Transit with seats for the band and windows. Mike or Peter drove it, while the equipment was in the box Transit, driven by me or Gerard. It was still just the seven of us on the road together, which when you look at the armies of crew that bands employ nowadays seems ludicrously small.

It was a four-hour crossing and we were bored stiff because there was nothing whatsoever to do. I found this box with life vests in it, and so we all got our vests on and posed for what has now become a famous picture of Genesis, all of us with our hair down past our shoulders, Mike drinking from a small bottle of *Mateus Rosé* because that's what we drank in those days, that or *Liebfraumilch*. I guess Strat had yet to sophisticate our drinking habits.

Nowadays when you go abroad you have satellite navigation that tells you precisely where to go and mobile phones or tablets with maps on them, but I really had no idea where we were heading in Belgium. I didn't even have a fold-out map. Furthermore, when we got to the venue, *if* we got to the venue, we hadn't a clue what the get in was going to be like either. I didn't absorb much from my very expensive education but one thing I did learn was how to speak a bit of French, so when the time came for needing directions I'd roll down a window and ask someone on the street. More importantly, when they responded in French telling me where to go I could understand. Phil, who was in the van with us so he could play his cassettes, was utterly gobsmacked. Believe it or not, he'd never met anyone who could speak a foreign language. When we got to the gig Phil told the others he couldn't believe Rich spoke French to this bloke. He was absolutely blown away. Of course Peter, Mike and Tony weren't impressed at all. After all, they had all been to Charterhouse too. Soon Peter was to become famous for introducing the songs in the appropriate language of whichever country we were in, something he still does to this day.

Mind you, they were all astonished when it dawned on us that we could go to a foreign country and, not only was the place, a club called Ferme V, packed to the roof, but the fans knew every note. It was unbelievable. While in England it was a very slow build-up, in Belgium it happened very suddenly, like a minor explosion as far as we were concerned. Another thing I remember is that we stayed in a three-star hotel, very comfy, and that Peter shared a room with me because he couldn't bear to share with Tony ever again, not after his experiences at the cottage.

Another thing I recall from our first visit to Belgium was that some bright spark realised in Brussels that we weren't very far from Luxembourg, where the radio station broadcast from. It was generally decided that this was too good an opportunity to miss, so lots were cast and it fell to me, Peter and Phil to set off there in the van, with all the gear, instead of driving to Ostend from Brussels and getting the ferry home with the others.

We headed off in the opposite direction, driving through a snowy winter's night to Luxembourg, to the Villa Louvigny. God knows how we managed it as this was after playing a gig, the whole set-up, sound check, gig, breakdown... how I had the stamina I'll never know. Nothing had been organised. We just showed up unannounced. I guess if we had tried to organise it we'd probably have been told not to come.

Kid Jenson was there, just him; I don't think there was a producer in a booth. It was the middle of the night, he was broadcasting and in we went. Nobody offered us a glass of water even, let alone a cup of coffee. Anyway, he started to do an interview and you could tell he was distinctly underwhelmed to see us. It's funny now to think that he had Peter Gabriel and Phil Collins arriving in the middle of the night in his studio and he wasn't really that excited about it. He told us he didn't have any of our records here. We didn't have any either but when it was all over and we were driving back Phil said he thought he saw Jenson open a drawer and there was a copy of *Trespass* in it. Then he shut the drawer again really quickly. Be that as it may, an interview was done but no music was played.

We got back in the van and headed back to Brussels and on to Ostend. I remember crawling up a hill in the wind and snow and having the illusion that we weren't moving at all. I was totally exhausted. Somehow we made it to the Dover ferry and home. Someone had got hold of a radio on the boat and the others had all listened. Reception was always really fuzzy on Radio Luxembourg but we all put up with because it was the only thing worth listening to. The only other person who heard it was Mike Rutherford's mother because she was the most wonderfully dedicated fan; there she was in bed in Farnham with her husband, the Captain, and the transistor radio under the pillow, just like a teenager.

Back in the UK, we soldiered on. On gig days the band used to meet up at Tony's flat in Bramham Gardens in Earls Court where he lived with Margaret. Peter still had the flat with Jill in Wandsworth, Steve lived with his parents in Ebury Bridge Road in Victoria and Mike also had a flat in London by this point. I would leave two hours before them, Phil having made his way up to Kilburn on the tube to get a ride with me.

We all lived in London on our £10 a week, which I think went up to £15 in 1971. All the money we earned at gigs I'd give it to Fred who operated a float system for all the Charisma bands.

I had a float of £100, and I'd keep receipts for petrol and things like equipment repairs and hand them over to him. Bookkeeping was important. The only bonus for me was the Green Shield stamps that I used to collect for the petrol and cash in for rubbishy gifts. Along the way the equipment was gradually improving, notably a bigger PA, all advanced to us by Charisma. Genesis never had a big cash advance to spend like bands do today, just sufficient for our needs, whether it was gear or rent or food. We weren't running at a profit and whatever money I scraped together from gigs would be set against the overall debt we were amassing.

The truth is that we all owed a huge debt of gratitude to Lindisfarne who were doing incredibly well, creaming in the cash for Charisma, and that's what Strat gave – or loaned – to Genesis. I don't think many people realise how much we all benefited from Lindisfarne's success. The Newcastle band were definitely Charisma's cash cow, making good money on the road, particularly at festivals where their sing-along songs went down especially well, and having hits like 'Meet Me On the Corner' (a No.5 in 1972) and 'Lady Eleanor' (No.3 the same year). Their second album *Fog On the Tyne* reached No.1 in the UK, and that pushed their debut album *Nicely Out Of Tune* into the charts two years after it was originally released.

I owed a personal debt to Lindisfarne, too, as I had an affair with one of the band's wives and what's more it was sanctioned by her husband. I was living in Hackney at the time and I'd become friendly with Lindisfarne's guitarist Simon Cowe and his wife Betsy. We'd hang out in the evening, have a spliff or two and listen to music. I was drawn to Betsy, the truth is I adored her. She was a teacher and because she didn't want to be known as Betsy Cowe she used her maiden name Gibson. Lindisfarne went on tour to Japan and during a discussion with Simon over the phone from Japan, she told him she wanted to have a fling with me and he said OK. I may be wrong but I imagine he was enjoying the attention of geisha girls in Japan at the time, so there was a green light in his mind for Betsy and me to get together. We had lots in common, particularly our interest in natural organic food and macrobiotics. At the time in London in the early 70s there were two American brothers, Craig and Greg Sams, who were the first to import organic food from the States. They set up a shop on Portobello Road called Ceres (now the Grain Shop) and among other things they published a monthly magazine called *Seed*. Betsy and I absolutely loved it. We used to read to each other in bed, thrilling descriptions of organic vegetables and brown rice. One of the Sams brothers, Craig, ended up starting Green & Blacks and eventually sold it to some big chocolate company for a fortune.

I guess I was simply doing my bit to make sure all the bands got on well. In some ways there's a tortoise and hare analogy between Genesis and Lindisfarne but it was their presence on the 'Six Shilling Tour' that brought in the fans, many of whom would be seeing Genesis for the first time. It was Strat's brilliant idea to promote three Charisma bands at once: us, our Geordie pals and Van Der Graaf Generator, another prog band who were developing a respectable cult following. Because Lindisfarne were topping the bill, we could play bigger tour venues and because the tickets cost just six shillings (30p in today's money) plenty of fans turned out, so those who came to see Lindisfarne also saw Genesis. I met someone recently whose dad did just that and came away completely converted to Genesis. He didn't even stay for Lindisfarne!

Charisma even organised a press coach for the show at the Brighton Dome, which might just have been the occasion when several music writers saw the band live for the first time. It was a novel idea, marvellous in its way and very far-sighted of Strat. Later on in the 70s Stiff Records did exactly the same thing with their Naughty Rhythms tour that featured Elvis Costello, Ian Dury and a few others.

Steve Hackett still remembers the 'Six Shilling Tour':

It went down very well and I remember meeting Chris Welch who liked us. He liked Phil particularly; I was talking to him about this recently. Phil bribed Chris with a half of bitter to write a good review. Suddenly the band was launched and I felt how kind you were and encouraging, Richard, when you said, 'I think you are alright for the band', 'cos I hadn't been at all sure. I was a bundle of nerves. My knees were knocking... volume pedal, sometimes people might be thinking, "How does he get that sound?" It wasn't technique, it was pure fear. And we were off doing sell outs on that six bob tour...

... It was a brilliant marketing idea of Strat's. The stable of acts known as Charisma were all on tour together and the acts were all very different from each other. Genesis was the warm-up band to the warm-up band at that time. The tour was pre-Mellotron time, pre-synth, pre-light show, pre-audience. Audiences had not decided whether they liked us or not. A lot of the time they would just go off to the bar because they didn't get it. There was no history. There was no one to hear us at that stage. But in a way that was very good. It was Lindisfarne who were going down the best in front of crowds in those days because they had this great sing-along show. 'We can have a wee wee, we can have a wet on the wall.' It was completely different but Genesis were very serious about getting it right.

Among the more unusual aspects of the show was Peter's bass drum which he would play while he was singing, pushing down the pedal with his foot at the same time and often playing a tambourine. This sometimes didn't sit well with Phil because Peter's timing was occasionally awry. Steve could sympathise with Phil's attitude. 'Imagine if they got another guitarist who's only got an E-string and he was playing that all night,' Phil muttered to Steve beneath his breath on more than one occasion.

In the summer of 1971 Genesis came off the road for a month and decamped to Strat's country house, Luxford in Crowborough, East Sussex, to write and prepare for recording their second album, *Nursery Cryme*. I can still see Strat now, like the fairy godfather he was. 'My dear boys, go to my country house for a few weeks,' he'd have said between sips of vodka. It made him appear terribly grand, like a Cabinet Minister, even though he rented it, charged to the company of course. I was joined by infamous Jenny from the house in Kilburn. Peter soon lusted after her causing Jill some measure of distress, so unfortunately, Jenny had to get back on the train to London to preserve the peace.

Genesis stayed at Luxford for about four weeks, writing all the songs that appeared on *Nursery Cryme* there, with me back on catering duty, cooking in a kitchen that was far better equipped than the one at Christmas Cottage. The gear was set up in a stable block and there were plenty of bedrooms for everyone. Strat would come down occasionally and bring friends with him, like Roy Flynn who ran the Speakeasy and once managed Yes, or other Charisma staff.

This time round we weren't dependent on Red Cross boxes from parents either. I still had a float and would do the food shopping for everyone, or drive up to London to collect the wages. It was a fun time, staying in a beautiful place in the country, with Jill and other band girlfriends sometimes joining us at weekends.

After leaving Luxford at the end of the summer, the band went back into the studio with John Anthony. They were at Trident again, which charged £60 an hour, but having rehearsed all the songs so well were able to record quite quickly. Genesis were always businesslike in that way, not ones to waste expensive studio time if it could be helped. The Beatles had the luxury of free studio time at Abbey Road, so they could write while they were recording, but this was an unusual indulgence not often enjoyed by anyone else.

The big song on the new album was 'The Musical Box' which I heard for the first time in a studio in West Hampstead, just off West End Lane, that belonged to John Mayall's brother Rod, who had been in Flaming Youth with Phil. I'd get there at nine in the morning to set up everything for a rehearsal, and they'd all arrive a couple of hours later and start writing and playing. I'd leave them to it and go off to Charing Cross Road to buy strings and tambourines and get mics repaired at the Shure depot, just the other side of Blackfriars Bridge. Peter would always throw them on the floor and break them, as if he was Pete Townshend or someone, a rare extravagance for Genesis. I'd get back to the studio at the end of the day after doing my rounds, maybe seeing Fred and Gail and all the rest and I remember that this particular day they said they wanted to play me something.

So I sat down and they played me 'The Musical Box' – I would have been the first person outside of the band to hear that song – and I was blown away. I knew immediately that it was a classic, that whole first bit based on an unusual tuning, chords of F sharp, and then a build-up to a crescendo, twin guitars and organ competing with Phil's drums as Peter screams above it all before the sudden staccato climax.

The song seemed to me to sum up the whole vitality of the group, and reinforced the pride I felt in being this non-playing but still essential cog in the Genesis wheel, a wheel that was spiralling ever upwards into a new cycle of creativity. We moved from Luxford in May to Trident Studios in the late summer and then back on the road in the autumn to play their new music for an ever increasing army of fans.

As the climax to 'The Musical Box' died away that day in the rehearsal studio and the five guys all looked towards me for a reaction, I could only grin back at them. Wow, I thought. Right then, I wouldn't have changed my life for all the tea in China.

Chapter 9

THE GRAND TOUR

*'Catholic countries throughout the world
subscribed to early Genesis. They liked the stories.
These were very religious countries
and it struck a chord deep within them.
I have to go on record and say it was theatrical.'*
Steve Hackett

Genesis were back on the road in the autumn of 1971 promoting
Nursery Cryme. Apart from the 'Six Shilling Tour' it was still
random dates here, there and everywhere, still working as hard
as we could. I don't ever remember more than a couple of days off
a week and anyway, a day without a gig was never a day off for me
because I was always chasing around, going to the office, picking
up wages, dealing with Fred, buying tambourines and strings,
getting microphones repaired. A roadie's work is never done.
I used to go to Charlie Foot's legendary drum shop in Golden
Square for Phil's sticks. Fortunately it was around the corner from
Brewer Street, where Charisma's office was located.

Aside from my rather liberated relationship with Betsy,
there wasn't much interaction between the bands on the label,
or even with other bands playing the same venues. They might
have appeared next to each other in the pages of *Melody Maker*
but they never saw each other because they were all out on the

road working. Not long ago, Tony Banks appeared on a Prog Rock Awards show and the presenter asked him what he thought about other prog bands like Yes, ELP, Jethro Tull and Pink Floyd. His reply was, 'We absolutely hated them. They were the competition.' (Tony's always been incredibly honest, often to his own disadvantage.) So this idea of them all being lovey-dovey prog groups together, all supporting and admiring one another was a complete fantasy. I know Tony wouldn't have admired Lindisfarne musically because their style was too harmonically simple for his taste, yet he couldn't not be impressed by the way they got the audience going.

Any rivalry between the bands didn't extend towards the road crews. There was certainly plenty of camaraderie among the roadies who worked for the bands on Charisma. We were all doing the same job, as well as we could. Van Der Graaf Generator had an outrageous pair called Crackie and Nodge. Crackie ended up becoming Strat's trusted driver. He was a largish, chronically asthmatic Welshman while Nodge, also Welsh, was a skinny little guy with a patch over one eye. They were chalk and cheese. At one of the gigs on the 'Six Shilling Tour' we could move the gear to and from the stage through a trap door that would have been used for special effects. Crackie, in his lovely Welsh accent, said something about how it was like being down the mines. Of course he'd never been near a coal mine in his life.

On that tour, just to ring the changes and alleviate the boredom that comes with staying in the same hotels and driving from one grimy northern town to another, we decided to swap passengers around in the vans. Two of the Van Der Graaf members, Guy Evans, the drummer, and Dave Jackson, the saxophone player, came with me in our van and from that day friendship grew between us. On another occasion, we needed to swap vans with them for some reason and it was pouring with rain, so I came up with this really clever idea of making the swap beneath the underpass at Paddington. We parked the vans back to back but slightly off kilter so you could still get into both vehicles and transfer all the gear by sliding it along the floors of one van into the other.

Gradually the gigs got bigger and better. The equipment was improving too. It was around this time that we got a multicore – a long cable for all the on-stage mics – and this meant that I could position myself with the mixing desk half way back in the audience. On *Foxtrot*, the album after *Nursery Cryme*, there's a picture of me in a top hat, taken at Tony and Margaret Banks's wedding. Peter wrote a caption that read: 'Faithful barefooted Richard, stage sound and sound friend'. I never wore shoes in those days. I didn't see the point and I was letting my freak flag fly.

There were ten or a dozen mics on stage to mix, certainly enough to mic up the drums. At one end of the multicore, there was a box into which they were all plugged; the cable then ran to the desk where it separated into more connections that plugged into the mixer. They were all numbered so you would know what was coming through what, and as the mixing process became more complex, it became more important for us to do a sound check before the show to get it all in balance. We always started with the drums and built the rest of the sound picture from there.

I taught myself to mix the sound on stage. I didn't find it hard. My reference point would have been the recordings, even though, as I said earlier, I thought the first two records lacked the power Genesis had when they played live. Nevertheless, I knew what the balance *should* be. Mostly, my preoccupation was driven by trying to get Peter's vocals to be audible through the instruments. He's never had a naturally powerful voice and has always struggled to be heard clearly at live shows. As our tours wore on, he would also inevitably tend to lose vocal strength. I would do what I could to compensate, but it was difficult getting the vocals out as much as I would have liked. Tony Banks didn't mind at all because he saw the vocals as being like another one of the instruments. This would always be an issue when they were mixing in the studio because Peter would always want the vocals up and Tony disagreed. Mind you, that's not an uncommon thing with groups: singers wanting to be heard and the rest not really caring. Look at the Stones. You often can't hear what Mick is singing but it doesn't matter at all, it's part of their style. I think that it also adds to the mystery.

Steve took care of most of the guitar parts and Mike, who was playing bass a bit on stage, would soon get a double-neck Rickenbacker, with bass and either 12-string or six-string guitar, that was specially made for him. He would switch between guitar and acoustic and bass pedals, which he got the following year at the time of *Foxtrot*. The lack of designated bass player was something unique to Genesis. Apart from The Doors, I can't think of any other bands that didn't have one.

One of our regular venues was Eel Pie Island, an eyot on the Thames near Twickenham with a footbridge that was just big enough to drive a small car across. The promoter there had a minivan so we would load it up – it would take three or four goes – and he would trundle the gear across. The hotel on the island was semi-derelict but it had a ballroom that was just about serviceable. I was amazed to discover that it had stages at either end. We performed there with Free, them at one end and us at the other. They did a set, we did a set, then they did another and we did another, all because we could leave the gear in place. Free were huge at the time, much bigger than Genesis, with a great bass player in Andy Fraser, and Paul Kossoff, a superb guitarist. Both are dead now, but what a band they were at the time.

After the gig I stashed our mics into a duffle bag with a drawstring to tighten it at the top. We used the mini for the larger pieces of equipment, quite possibly putting a strain on the footbridge. It was left to me to carry the last few smaller pieces over the bridge including the bag of mics. Somehow, the top mic fell out and landed in the river with an ominous plop. It's still there. I certainly didn't go in after it. This is the sort of incident that a roadie wishes he could forget.

It was always a slow build for Genesis. Strat, with his indefatigable belief in the band, was always looking for ways to promote his beloved protégés. He hit upon the idea of getting Keith Emerson, who had just formed Emerson, Lake and Palmer, to write a piece endorsing Genesis for publication in the music press. Keith wrote something along the lines of, 'One day Genesis are going to be big and one day you're going to wish you got in on the ground floor.' *Nursery Cryme* didn't set the world alight but live it was terrific, particularly 'The Musical Box'. It was a very well structured song and people used to go nuts at the end. Just last year Steve Hackett was doing his Genesis revisited show at the Royal Albert Hall and he played 'The Musical Box'. I was in tears because the response was exactly the same as it had been with Genesis all those years before. Fifty years had gone by but the song still generated the same strong reaction in the crowd.

In retrospect, the most important events for Genesis during 1972 were the two first Italy tours, one in April and the next in August. Sandwiched between them were intense writing sessions of what would become *Foxtrot*. These took place down at Luxford and at a dance studio on Shepherds Bush Road. Once again Phil surprised us with an unexpected connection. Having attended the Barbara Speake Acting School as a young boy, subsequently appearing as the artful dodger in the 1960 London stage production of *Oliver!* and as an extra in *A Hard Day's Night*, he was able to introduce us to the Una Billings Dance Studio and it was here that 'Supper's Ready' began to take shape. At 23 minutes, it took up the whole of the second side of *Foxtrot* – a big concept piece.

Tony Banks has gone on record as saying it's just a bunch of bits that they glued together, and in a way it was, but it is still an amazing piece of music:

That was an overall Genesis thing. Some of the pieces were made up from bits written by individuals, and the trouble was that we wanted to change the keys to make them fit. A prime example was 'Supper's Ready' where 'Willow Farm', which is in A flat major, was meant to lead on to a little flute melody in A minor. So we had to get between the two and we weren't going to change 'Willow Farm' and I wasn't going to change the flute melody because I'd written it on the guitar and it was open strings, so we had to travel through these weird chords in between. When it comes out it's a totally natural change, and you've got there without realising it. There's another one at the end of that section, of course, which goes into 'Apocalypse in 9/8' which is a diminished chord, but on that occasion it was more like, you've built up this big expectancy and you think it's going to be a major chord but it's another chord, an F sharp minor which you are not expecting, and that's an incredibly exciting chord change.

Tony explains further:

You think it's going to resolve in a different way and then it goes into an unlikely chord and suddenly it's very aggressive. I did that because I wanted to get to this F sharp minor change. This is quite technical but F sharp minor, a minor 6th was from a piece I learned at school called 'Night In May' by Selim Palmgren, and it had a chord change in it and I always thought it was a great sound and we must use that. So I alternated between those chords before going into the solo. I'd written the thing and I wanted to try and keep it in that key and it produced quite interesting results, [so] rather than just everything being in the same key I made these adjustments, particularly in something like 'Supper's Ready' which is a very episodic piece. This was new. It was something I did in my own songs, so the chorus and the verse were in different keys. Holland Dozier Holland did that all the time on songs like 'Baby I Need Your Loving'. It shifts and you think, 'That's great.' The change itself is so good that it makes whatever you do afterwards sound really great. I did a lot of that in my own writing.

Foxtrot was recorded at the Island Records studios in Basing Street and instead of John Anthony, John Burns was brought in to produce it. At last they had made an album where I felt that the production did justice to their sound.

When they'd finished rehearsing 'Supper's Ready', they did the same thing they'd done with 'The Musical Box', inviting me to come and listen. As before, I'd been chasing around picking up wages and buying drumsticks, all the mundane tasks of my job. I then went down to the studio and sat and listened. Twenty-three minutes later my mind was blown; this was the most unbelievable piece of music I'd ever heard them play and happily, John Burns did a good job of capturing it on record.

The sessions for *Foxtrot* were bracketed by the two Italian tours. None of us really appreciated how well the band was going down in Italy, at least not until we got there and saw it for ourselves. Before leaving I raised my eyebrows a bit when I noticed that the scheduled gigs were going to be those *palazzo dello sport* places, medium indoor basketball arenas that were bigger than anywhere we'd played in the UK. I guess the Italian promoter knew what he was doing but it was still a surprise.

Bigger gigs meant we needed a bigger PA and that meant a bigger van. Before we went I got back in touch with our friend Reg King and told him we were going to need a three-tonner, which is the largest truck you can drive without a Heavy Goods Vehicle licence. Reg didn't have a three-tonner so he subcontracted one from Godfrey Davis, the truck hire company. I went to Alperton to pick it up and Reg met me there, showing up on cue in his Cadillac. He said, 'I haven't told them you're taking it abroad. If anything happens, bury it. Just leave it over there.'

Of course I had the *carnet* and all the rest of it but God knows if I was properly insured, probably not. Reg wasn't one to worry about such details. The truck was easy enough to drive but when I first climbed into the cab, the one thing I couldn't do was let the handbrake off. I didn't recognise the unusual rod that came out of the dashboard. You had to pull and then turn to release it. I couldn't figure it out. When the guy at Godfrey Davis asked me if I'd ever driven one before, I had brazenly replied, 'Of course. No trouble, mate.' I managed to get it started but he had to show me how to work the handbrake. 'It wasn't like this on the last one I drove,' I insisted, never having driven one before. He gave me an odd look, probably not liking the length of my hair and my patent ignorance. I doubt Reg had mentioned that the truck was being used by a rock band.

The other trick I had to learn was how to bleed the brakes when you parked up for the night. There was a big cylinder underneath the cab and it would make a loud hissing noise when you bled it. When you then started the engine it pumped up again. In those days I could still park it outside wherever I was living, so there was never an issue with what to do with the truck at night. As far as I'm aware we didn't even have insurance for the gear that was left in the van, unattended of course. We didn't worry about any of those details. It was an anonymous Godfrey Davis rental van, could have been full of anything – office furniture, fruit & veg or building materials. Eventually we bought our own three-tonner, with a cream cab and a brown box, quite a distinctive livery. Nobody would have known it contained Genesis's priceless equipment.

So off we went to Italy, across the Channel, down through France and over the Alps. The band went in a van with actual seats and windows, accompanied by Paul Conroy from Charisma's booking agency. There'd been some changes in the road crew by now. Gerard had gone and another old friend of mine called Paul Davidson, a school friend of one of my Millfield friends, Michael Reed, had taken over. He was at a loose end and became a great roadie mate. It's funny to think that we were still recruiting roadies from the ranks of my school friends rather than professionals. That would come later.

So the conquest of Italy began. I remember driving down the Valle D'Aosta to Turin, Milan and Brescia, with breathtaking mountain scenery all the way. The promoter was called Maurizio Salvatore and he had arranged about 15 gigs for us, a substantial tour. We went down as far as Naples but no further south. The tour finished with a show on the outskirts of Rome. In those days there was a lot of political unrest in Italy that used to focus on rock gigs. This meant the police wouldn't allow performances in the centre of towns, so you were always 20 miles or so outside in some sports arena.

On a typical day we'd get to the gig and it was wonderful for me because the venue would be completely empty and we would be met by a stage with huge loading doors at the back. We'd reverse in, up to the stage and out came the equipment, straight on to the stage, no carrying it along corridors or up the stairs, plus there were all these agreeably willing fans who would help with the gear. It made my job so much easier. The band then used the empty van as a dressing room. We'd get into the venue at around 11 in the morning, set up and then do a proper sound check, allowing plenty of time to get it right. These places were like cathedrals. You clapped your hands and you'd still hear the sound 12 seconds later, reverberating around the space. In some ways, mixing the sound was a bit academic – it was just swirling around – but it didn't matter as the fans really loved it. After we'd set up and done the soundcheck, it would be about 1 or 1.30 p.m. and Maurizio would say, 'OK. *Mangiamo.*' He always knew where the best restaurants were, so off we'd go for a huge lunch. We quickly learned how to eat in the style: first a pasta starter, often a scrumptious plate of incredible homemade spaghetti with a delicious sauce, then a slab of meat, no veg, maybe a bit of salad, and then a desert like tiramisu. We also discovered fantastic wines to wash it all down with, so by the end of lunch, typically about four in the afternoon, we'd be absolutely stuffed and out of it. We'd go back to the hotel, shut the blinds down with proper shutters to create complete darkness, collapse into bed and sleep like the dead for two hours and then get up and do the gig. Life was good. We would return to the sports arena and it would be packed with 5000 fans, sometimes more, especially on the second tour when we might have up to 10,000 waiting to hear us.

I've often wondered why Genesis appealed to the Italians as much as they did. We met the Italian music writer and photographer, Armando Gallo, on these first tours and he cottoned on to us early and became a big supporter, eventually writing several books about the band. I think Italians appreciated the emotional content of Genesis music. It was romantic, like opera, and the songs were resembled long suites. A fast and furious passage would often bring people to their feet. Being such avid fans the Italians had bought and absorbed all the records; this crowd knew every note and nuance of the songs. It was extraordinary really. We'd never experienced anything like it. There I was at the mixing desk in the middle of the audience and they were all clapping, a wonderful experience to see my boys being so understood and appreciated. The fans loved it all and gave the band standing ovations at the end of every show. It did wonders for their confidence and all five guys, Peter, Mike, Tony, Steve and Phil, have never forgotten the warmth of their early following in Italy, or its importance in their development as a band. I hope we paid our debt of gratitude by playing well for them.

Steve has another theory as to why Genesis were so popular in Italy:

> *I think it has something to do with Catholicism. I think it's to do with the theological nature of many of the songs. And it was partly that track 'Fountains Of Salmacis' that audiences in the rest of the world didn't understand at the time. That track... they got it immediately. I think they understood it because of the Greco-Roman connection. Catholic countries throughout the world subscribed to early Genesis. They liked the stories. These were very religious countries and it struck a chord deep within them. I have to go on record and say it was theatrical. I know that the others tend to distance themselves from that era but when they look at the early model they can't understand why those albums still sell so well. But I feel that I do understand it.*

On the second Italian tour we had a bit of a problem on the way over because we didn't know that in Europe they have a lot of extra bank holidays, religious holidays that were Saints' days. The border was closed to us, not for cars but for trucks with a *carnet*, and we got stuck somewhere in the French Alps. Of course back then there were no mobile phones, no ATM bank machines, no credit cards, no internet, nothing. We only had enough cash to get us over to Italy, maybe to buy us a couple of meals, but no reserve and there we were stuck in the foothills of the French Alps until the border opened in a couple of days. So we retreated into the hills nearby. By this time there were a couple more roadies, one being Adrian Selby, Gerard's younger brother who had joined us straight from school and eventually ended up taking my place.

We slept rough under the truck and the next morning washed in a fountain in the middle of a tiny Alpine village.

All this meant we were about two days late getting to Rimini where the band were all waiting for us. Hearing nothing, they obviously thought the worst – that we'd driven off the edge of a cliff somewhere and had all perished. They were visibly relieved to see us but also a bit pissed off. Margaret Banks gave me a real dressing down. 'Don't you dare do that again,' she said to me. 'You put us through hell.'

The other addition to the crew was a professional sound mixer to work our new mixing desk. He showed me how to use it, but by this time I had graduated to becoming Genesis tour manager, the guy with the briefcase who travelled with the band, looked after admin and no longer humped the gear. Until then I was just a general do-everything roadie, so you could say that I'd been promoted, in recognition of my long and devoted service. Not before time, though it soon made me realise that having reached this stage, maybe my horizons were beginning to expand, possibly beyond the world of Genesis.

MY BOOK OF GENESIS

Trellick Tower, London W10, designed by
Ernö Goldfinger. My flat was fourth from
the top, on the right-hand-side.

The houses that
Ernö Goldfinger built
in Willow Road, Hampstead
that so enraged the neighbours,
including the family of
Ian Fleming.

Amusing ourselves on a
long Channel crossing en
route to one of our first
overseas gigs (Brussels).

Mike Rutherford standing
at the back, middle row:
Tony Banks, Peter Gabriel
and Steve Hackett;
kneeling at front: RPM
and Phil Collins.

Sometimes at the sound check
I would set up a mic at the
mixing desk so Peter Gabriel
could check the balance.

This was taken in 1973 on
an early US tour.

Backstage after Peter's show
at Knebworth, 1977.

RPM, Peter Gabriel and Tony Smith, with
thanks to Armando Gallo for the picture.

A bit of car fun with yours truly – thank you
Tony Levin for the photo.

More car fun with Peter Gabriel - thank you
Tony Levin for the picture.

Photo from the inside of the album cover for *Foxtrot*.

From left: Tony Banks, Steve Hackett and RPM

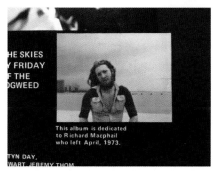

The dedication from the *Genesis Live* album of 1973.

The picture was taken by Margaret Banks on the shore of Lake Michigan, Chicago.

Tony Levin snapped Peter and me in the phone box moments before our arrest as terrorists in St Gallen, Switzerland.

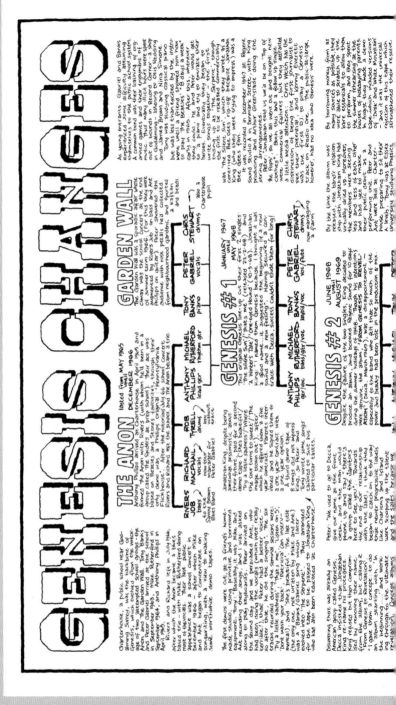

Courtesy of Pete Frame: Rock Family Trees

Chapter 10

THE GUY IN
THE TOP HAT

*To my horror, I wasn't allowed to touch any of the
equipment because the venue was all unionised; no
one had told me. There were all these union guys there
and I had to tell them what to do.*

Genesis went to America for the first time in December 1972,
a mini tour that took us to Boston and New York. Strat had signed
the band to Buddha Records in the US, a label run by a guy called
Neil Bogart who like so many Americans in the record business
was a real character – a ducker and diver as we might say in the
UK. Also we had an American manager, another larger than life
character, called Ed Goodgold who had previously managed
Sha Na Na, the slightly tongue-in-cheek 50s revival band who had
been a hit at Woodstock. They were about as far removed from
Genesis as possible. Ed had studied to be a rabbi but somehow
got sidetracked into music management. In the string of colourful
characters that I met in the business he was a gem, a wise and
funny guy.

Strange though it may seem now, we went all the way to
America for just two gigs on that initial trip. First was a warm-up
at the prestigious Brandeis University in Boston, followed by a
charity affair at the Lincoln Center in New York. We had no flight
cases in those days. We just drove the van to Heathrow and linked

up with Rocket Cargo, the company that became the go-to blokes for bands to ship their gear around the world. We simply loaded all our equipment into a cargo bay, it was shoved into the hold of the plane and then eight hours later, by some miracle, it came out the other end.

Like most people, I will never forget the first time I flew to New York. By this time I was living in Stratford East. I'd moved from Kilburn to West Hampstead and from there out to Stratford where we were able to rent a house very cheaply as it was still an absolute wasteland in those days. I remember getting on the Central Line and looking at all the commuters, thinking to myself that they were on their way to some boring office job whereas I was on my way to New York! Back in 1972, it was still pretty unusual to go to America. It wasn't the holiday destination it is now, and relatively speaking, it was very expensive to fly there. So sitting there on the tube opposite a phalange of commuters was another of those moments when I couldn't help thinking that if it weren't for Genesis and for music, I could have been living that life, the one my parents had planned, going to work every day in a suit and tie. From where I sat it seemed a desperately dull existence.

We flew Pan Am in a jumbo jet. It's hard to describe how surreal this experience felt for the first time. Even landing at JFK, passing through immigration and making our way into the City was unbearably exciting. We were booked into the Gorham Hotel, which is on 55th Street around the back of Carnegie Hall. Imagine our joy at discovering that the famous Carnegie Deli was just round the corner and would deliver salt beef sandwiches to our hotel rooms. Those first few hours in New York were overwhelming. To think that I started the day in Stratford and ended up in the heart of Manhattan devouring an impossibly large salt beef sandwich from the Carnegie Deli! Jet travel still amazes me and always will.

I went with the two other roadies and Fred Munt from Charisma. I guess Strat sent Fred over because he'd been to America before. We had to get a truck, drive out to the airport along Rockaway Boulevard – so much more evocative a name than Cromwell Road – and collect the gear. Unfortunately, the Mellotron was in a very sorry state as we hadn't been able to pack it properly. Nowadays it would have its own specially built flight case costing a fortune but not back then.

It was the middle of winter and bitterly cold up on the East Coast. The tops of the buildings were hidden by clouds but never having seen truly high skyscrapers we didn't know what we were missing. The band arrived and Ed Goodgold, who accompanied us, thought we would feel more at home if he took us to a restaurant called The Chef & Brewer. It was meant to be like an English pub but was nothing like one at all. Ed thought he would ease us in gently but we would have enjoyed a real American 'joint' far more. By now it was 8 p.m. in New York, the equivalent of one in the morning in London, so I didn't know whether I was coming or going.

Brandeis University was arranged as a warm-up gig so we drove up to Boston, a similar distance as London to Newcastle. When we arrived, still reeling from jetlag, we set up the Mellotron and discovered that it was in even worse shape than we had realised. There was no way of getting it repaired and no time to source a replacement. Luckily, the Brandeis guys who were helping us were all science students. We all knew that the voltage in America was 110, as opposed to 220 in Europe, but they figured out that the problem was to do with the number of hertz in the electric current. So these wonderful guys set to and made a hertz converter in a big box. We also had to jam bits of wood down inside the recently mangled frame of the Mellotron. If we had done that gig anywhere else, we wouldn't have been able to use it but they got it working and the show went on.

It was now time to head back to New York for the real show at the Philharmonic Hall, now called the Alice Tully Hall and part of the Lincoln Center. I remember meeting Neil Bogart from Buddha Records for the first time in his office somewhere in Midtown; he was another character straight out of central casting with a big cigar. Also part of the new set-up was a guy with the spectacular name of Regis Boff. How I grew to love these American names.

With Fred being there too, we had plenty of support. The gig had attracted a huge amount of publicity since it was a charity show put on by WNEW, the top New York FM rock radio station. They had done a huge build-up for the band – 'the great Genesis from London' kind of thing.

Setting off from the Gorham Hotel with Tony and Mike in the rental car, I quickly proved myself to be a novice New York driver. Coming out of 55th Street, I turned left in the direction in which the traffic was flowing and before realising it had gone 30 blocks in the wrong direction. What I needed to do was to go over to Eighth Avenue and drive uptown to Columbus Circle, which in heavy rush hour traffic took ages. We finally got there but very late.

At this point there was nothing to do but leave the car outside the stage door and put the flashers on. We went in and I didn't give the car another thought because this was such an important gig and everyone was there, a host of people who were crucial to Genesis in America. There was another unexpected problem. When we finally got a chance to do a soundcheck, there was a buzz on the PA that I couldn't eliminate; I wasn't allowed to touch any equipment because the Hall was unionised. None of my mentors had mentioned this. I remember all these union guys running around with me telling them what to do. 'Take this speaker and put it there. Now, get this amp and put it here. Now take its cover off.' We weren't even allowed to plug anything in. It was mind blowing for me, being so used to setting up Genesis myself and knowing how it should be done.

Eventually we got set up and the gig happened but it wasn't great. In fact, it was really bad. I met up with the band in the wings when they came off stage and we all took the lift up to the dressing room. Mike expressed how pissed off we all were by throwing his Rickenbacker bass on the floor in frustration. Not like Mike at all. We thought it had been a disaster. At that moment it seemed that way.

After the show Buddha Records had organised a reception at the Tavern on the Green, a restaurant in the middle of Central Park. It was only then that I remembered that I had to deal with the abandoned car. To my astonishment, when I came out hours later it was still there by the stage door but the battery was flat because I'd left the flashers on. Being an automatic, I couldn't bump start it unless I got up to 30 mph. Amazingly I found a cab driver who was willing to push me that fast with the bumpers of his cab. Even though we achieved the requisite take-off speed, it still wouldn't start so he pushed me to a gas station over on Tenth Avenue where they put a charger on it and got it going again. I missed the reception but that night I learned how kind and helpful New Yorkers can be.

The gig turned out not to be the disaster that we had all thought. *Cashbox* magazine came out with an unbelievably positive review even though we all still insisted that it was the lousiest gig they'd ever played. I sometimes think that someone somewhere was watching over us – or maybe that formidable pair, Ed Goodgold and Neil Bogart, slipped something into the reviewer's drink at the reception. I wouldn't have put it past them.

We flew home for Christmas the next day. Before going out to the airport, I made a dash to the famous FAO Schwartz toy store to buy Christmas presents for my niece and nephew, Jo and Andrew.

Between the two tours of Italy in 1972 the gigs kept coming. I remember going to Brussels for a TV show in April and to the Great Western Festival near Lincoln at the end of May. That festival was almost certainly the biggest audience that Genesis had played to up to that point. Unfortunately, it started to rain just as the band came on. It was only a shower but while they were playing their jangly acoustic guitar music, the entire audience was wrestling with pieces of plastic to shelter under. It was not a wow, but what made it worse was that Status Quo came on immediately after us and of course, just blasted away with their 12-bar boogie music and set the place alight. We played on the Saturday afternoon but I stayed on to see The Beach Boys who were top of the bill the next night. Sadly Brian Wilson wasn't able to tour with them that time but they compensated way more than adequately by adding Rikki Fataar and Blondie Chaplin from South Africa. I remember sitting in the enclosure at the front with Elkie Brooks and

Allan White, the three of us just being together, enjoying a joint or two and singing at the top of our voices to all those classic Beach Boys songs. Some might say that Genesis wasn't really a festival band though they did eventually top the bill at Reading.

Peter's dressing up began late that summer on September 28th at a gig in a boxing arena in Dublin called the National Stadium. Unbeknownst to all of us Peter had acquired a fox's head mask and had borrowed a red dress from Jill. The image was similar to the one Paul Whitehead had designed for the sleeve of *Foxtrot* which featured a woman with a fox's head. I can't remember whether he drew it because of Peter wearing the dress or whether Peter wore the dress because of the sleeve, but either way he surprised the hell out of us all. During 'The Musical Box' there's quite a long instrumental solo, after which he came back on stage in this outfit. Tony Banks would never have agreed to it and he was horrified. There he was playing the keyboard, minding his own business, and Peter materialises in front of him in a red dress and fox's head. He finished the song and the place went berserk. It brought the house down. So of course it was a *fait accompli*. Tony couldn't complain after that.

I'm sure Jill helped him with this bit of stagecraft. After all, it was her dress though I'm surprised Peter could get into it. Maybe she altered it for him. It was also around this time that he cut his hair strangely, shaving off a small triangle at the front, so he looked a bit like an alien. He'd cottoned on to the fact that it just wasn't enough to simply play good music. You had to stand out to get people's attention, so he started to get more and more outrageous on stage. Of course, it also made the music press sit up and take notice. The huge flower mask came with 'Supper's Ready'. There's a moment in the song when he sings 'a flower' and on went the mask for the rest of the song. Batwings became the signature for 'Watcher Of the Skies', the opening track on *Foxtrot*. All through this period Peter was becoming more and more noticeable on stage. Once he'd set out his stall in Dublin, there was no stopping him.

Tony, not one for public displays, thought the music was all that was necessary but I think deep down even he probably had to admit that it helped. Certainly *he* wasn't about to dress up. In a recent documentary about Genesis, Chester Thompson said that when he told his friends in America that he was joining Genesis their universal reaction was, 'You what? They'll make you dress up in crazy costumes!' Of course it was only ever Peter. Tony never compromised on that issue. The biggest concession he ever made was to wear a white shirt when they were playing on a white stage. Even he realised that the lights looked so much better if everything was white: the instruments, keyboards, floor, background, everything except, of course, Peter. The costumes really came into their own for *The Lamb Lies Down On Broadway*, which included a song called 'The Slipper Man'. Peter had had a costume made which was made up of boils and pustules, supposedly representing a sexually transmitted disease. But I'm getting ahead of myself...

Foxtrot actually got into the charts, reaching No. 12 in the UK in October 1972. The next album, *Genesis Live*, was recorded at the Free Trade Hall in Manchester and De Montfort Hall in Leicester later that year. The band dedicated the album to me and on the back of the sleeve there's a photograph of me that Margaret Banks took on the beach in Chicago, by the shores of Lake Michigan. This was on our first proper American tour, when we played the Aragon Ballroom in April 1973. The caption read 'Dedicated to Richard Macphail who left in April 1973'. To this day, I still run into fans who firmly believe that this was a discreet reference to my untimely death. They seem greatly relieved to find me alive!

The band was beginning to go down well in America. Just like in the UK, a following developed slowly. The fans didn't become impatient with Peter's little stories; they loved eccentric Englishmen. Peter was a bit like Ian Anderson in that respect, though at that time, Jethro Tull were far ahead of us in terms of popularity. Peter's stories also attracted the attention of the film director William Friedkin who made his name with *The French Connection* in 1971. He was working on *The Exorcist* when he got in touch. He'd seen a mini-story that Peter had written which was printed on the back of the live album. Friedkin read it and probably thought this was an interesting guy, someone he could work with. In the end, nothing came of it but it would play a small part in future upheavals.

The good relationship within the band was maintained as 1972 gave way to 1973. They were sounding better, going down better and the gigs were getting bigger. I remember we played the Rainbow in Finsbury Park in early February and the place was packed. This once famous venue had its first heyday as the Finsbury Park Astoria where The Beatles played a whole Christmas season – 16 nights in December and January of 1963/64. It then went on to become the Odeon before being revived as a music venue by Bill Graham and company who had launched the famous Fillmore venues in America. The Rainbow was inaugurated by The Who in 1971, but really hit the headlines the next month when Frank Zappa sustained serious injuries from falling off the stage during his performance.

Genesis's Rainbow gig was a real breakthrough for the band, a complete sell out with a standing ovation at the end. Photographer Barrie Wentzell took a picture of Peter in his flower headdress and it appeared on the front page of *Melody Maker*. In his review headed 'Genesis genius' Chris Welch wrote:

> *Genesis received such an ovation at London's Rainbow Theatre that it visibly moved this usually unflappable group. For twelve long minutes the audience cheered its appreciation for a stunning performance by the band. The musical fare will have been well familiar to the fans. From 'Watcher Of the Skies' to 'The Musical Box' to 'The Knife', each piece was a masterpiece of sustained invention, tempered by taste and skill as the various musicians sublimated their talents to create a vast range of tone colours and moods.*

The summer and autumn of 1973 was all about *Selling England By the Pound*, the album that many fans consider to be the best that this line-up of Genesis ever made. In spite of all this success, or maybe because of it, things were stirring in my heart. I was reaching a turning point… things were changing.

Chapter 11

WHY I LEFT GENESIS

---

*I felt they had reached a stage where they could
carry on without me. In a sense my job had been to
help them get to that place. That's how it felt to me;
I had done my job up to this point and
could do no more.*

When Peter left Genesis in August 1975 headlines hit the music press and fans were left reeling. No such pandemonium occurred when I decided to leave – but that's hardly surprising. Roadies, even those who have graduated from carrying amps to briefcases, are the unsung heroes of the rock trade and always will be. We accept our lot and sometimes bask in the reflected glory of our employers. But we don't make headlines when we quit.

So why did I go? This is a question I am still asked all these years later. I had been with Genesis since 1969, before anyone knew who they were, and in the spring of 1973 I came to the realisation that I didn't really have a life of my own. I had no space for a relationship, for learning new skills, for even a hobby. Although I was travelling a lot, it was all dictated by the demands of the group. This feeling crept up on me – the knowledge that I'd been with the band for five long years without a break. I was 22 and effectively managing them. Strat, their nominal manager, also ran their record company and therefore couldn't fully devote his time to managing Genesis. I knew they would never kick me out but I had my doubts about my own ability to become their full-time manager and take them to the next level. A certain lack of self-confidence began to creep in. I was a bit nervous about the future because I could see, especially that night at the Rainbow, that this was going somewhere, somewhere far beyond what we had ever imagined back at Christmas Cottage.

What's more, I knew at this point that they wouldn't collapse if I left. It may sound arrogant but I'd never had that certainty before. I felt they had reached a plateau from where they could carry on without me. In a sense my job had been to help them get to that place, with some help from others obviously. That's how it felt to me; I had done my job up to this point and could do no more. I had always wanted the world to know what a great band they were. With *Foxtrot* sounding so good and with the increasing success of the live shows, I knew it was going to happen for them and happen big. The world was now seeing and hearing what I had hoped and worked for.

Mike understood:

I remember thinking that the time had come for Richard to explore other things, the bigger picture. He could see the pattern stretching ahead – album, tour, album, tour – and I felt that he had come to a time in his life when he wanted to cast his net wider.

Tony also says:

By then we could cope with it. Obviously you'd been part of it from the beginning so it was a big thing for you to leave. Perhaps you wanted to go further than Genesis could give you.

Phil is clear about the band's dynamics:

That original configuration of people was unique. It was quite logical to think that if anything changed with this we would be fucked. If anyone was to leave, including Richard, doing their particular jobs, whether it was throwing the stuff in the back of the van or banging the WEM Audiomaster so that it sounded like thunder, then we'd all be in trouble. It was the chemistry of people. It's not just the job one does, it's the other things that make it almost more important. You don't just want five guys who can simply play the right notes all the time and take no risks. It's the personalities that make up the whole, and I think Richard's role in that was... someone who came in with constructive criticism.

Speaking to me from his home in Florida in late 2016, after he'd been in the UK to promote his autobiography, *Not Dead Yet*, Phil added:

If after the show you said, 'Tonight wasn't so great,' then we'd say, 'Well that's what Rich thinks so it must be true... it wasn't so great then.' We kind of believed each other. Then it started to change, and I don't think anyone of us believed the later crew guys when they came back and said it sounded great. Whereas if YOU said it, we did believe it. It was one of those early chemical mixes.

Steve has the last word on the subject:

You were chief cook, sound mixer, bottle washer. There was nothing you wouldn't do... consigliore, therapist and midwife. You talked me down many times. I was thinking, 'I'm gonna leave' but you'd say, 'No, no you are the right guy for the job.' I'd be thinking, 'Am I up to this?' and I didn't know until the second album that they actually liked my playing.

I had no idea what to do next but I did know that somewhere there was something lacking. I was discovering that I wanted more of what I called 'a spiritual life'. I had found out about Findhorn, a spiritual community in the north east of Scotland, where people seeking an alternative lifestyle had set up life in a caravan park outside the town of Forres on the Moray Firth. They had little money so they had to grow their own vegetables. By communicating with the plant spirits and following their instructions, they began to cultivate famously enormous vegetables and soon became a point of light for New Age seekers from all over the world. The vegetables were soon superseded by tales of a community which was really approaching life in a different way. I knew I wanted to go there.

Not long after I'd left the band, they were playing at the Free Trade Hall in Manchester, which like Leeds was a Genesis stronghold in the north of England. Peter and the others were making their way back to the stage door after having had something to eat in the city when a young woman came up to him as a fan and started talking. He probably asked where she was from and she replied 'Findhorn'. 'My friend Richard is really interested in what's going on there,' Peter told her and he took her details and passed them on to me. Soon afterwards I went up there and we connected – in the fullest sense of the word.

It was the very early days of Findhorn with maybe only between 50 and 100 people living there. I contacted Peter Caddy, the founder, and told him I wanted to join. After talking to me and getting a sense of my life, he said, 'You're not ready. Come back in a year.' But I never did. I was truly interested in New Age thinking and was seeking a different lifestyle.

Meanwhile Adrian Selby had taken over my role with the band, after which Tony Smith came on the scene and became their first proper manager. Tony and his father John were the UK's top promoters at the time and they were promoting Genesis concerts. According to Genesis legend, Tony and Mike were in a hotel in Alderley Edge, in the posh part of Cheshire where all the footballers now live, south of Manchester. They got talking and between them, hatched the idea of Tony managing the group. I think Smithy – he hates being called that but we all did – was fed up with doing the promoting bit and spotted an opportunity. Of course I was out of the picture but in hindsight it was the best thing that could have happened to them at that stage in their career. If I was the glue that helped the fledgling band stick together, then Tony Smith was the concrete that cemented everything in place.

By this time I'd moved into a squat in Freston Road, Notting Hill with my friend Rivers Job from Charterhouse. Eight of us took over two Victorian terraced houses, knocking them together so that we each had our own rooms plus a communal kitchen. Once again, in time-honoured tradition, I was given a vehicle by the aunt of my Millfield friend Philip Black, nephew of the famous impresario Lew Grade. In what I came to realise was an incredibly sweet gesture, Lew's wife Kathy (Lady Grade) gave me a Ford transit that had belonged to ATV. It featured a platform on top for mounting a camera, the sort of vehicle that would have driven along next to the Grand National while Julian Wilson rattled off his famous commentaries.

Equipped with the transit, I became part of an organisation called Gentle Ghost, a collective based in a building at the corner of Norland Road near the Shepherd's Bush roundabout. It was founded by a wonderfully inspired and somewhat crazy guy called Hugh Berger, who later wrote a book about it. One of its chapters was called 'Miranda's Friends' after my friend Miranda Davies who lived off Ladbroke Grove. When Miranda got involved, I joined up and one by one many others we knew jumped in.

Gentle Ghost functioned as a sort of alternative work agency, run by a motley crew of 'phone answerers' who arranged jobs on a Robin Hood basis, charging more for the relatively wealthy – often people in the arts who supported the project – and less, or even sometimes nothing, for the poor. Whenever anyone mentions Ghost these days, they immediately tend to think of the removal department, which is still a going concern, but this was really only the commercial end. There was also a help and advice section, which we all volunteered for, dealing with housing, health and drug issues as well as bizarre requests such as how to find a goat for a circus! We had strong links with Release, the well-known organisation set up in 1967 to help young people with drug related legal problems.

Besides doing the van removals, I eventually set up and ran an organic vegetarian café on the ground floor, which became very successful. All the money we earned was in common, which meant no one made a profit and each only took what they needed to cover their expenses. Another important aspect of Gentle Ghost was the training department where people learned skills such as carpentry, plumbing and electrics, so that they could become self-sufficient, useful members of the community.

For a while Gentle Ghost was the central focus of my life. I was earning a good living from removals. All a landlord needed to do was put a few sticks of furniture in a flat and the tenant had no security of tenure. All people owned were a few boxes of records and books, some plastic bags and a suitcase for their clothes. Moving house was easy. Very few of us actually possessed anything like beds, tables, sofas or wardrobes.

They always say that the most traumatic things in life are the death of a parent, losing a job or moving house so I was often meeting people at their most vulnerable. When we arrived the good customers would have practically everything they owned piled up on the pavement; I would rock up, throw everything into the back of the van and off I'd go. The bad ones would still be in bed with nothing packed at all. 'Oh man, is it Saturday already? Oh, really sorry man,' foreseeing the hippie character Neil, played years later by Nigel Planer in *The Young Ones*.

Strange as it may seem, I didn't regard this as being a comedown after my years with Genesis. Living in a squat and being part of Gentle Ghost, I was following the thread of my interest in community life, which had been sparked during my months on the kibbutz. I worked with Ghost for three years while staying in touch with my friends from Genesis all that time. I'd even return to work with them if an emergency cropped up.

One such emergency occurred when their lighting technician, Les Adey, was busted and couldn't leave the country. Genesis were all set to go on tour in the US in 1974 to promote *Selling England By the Pound* which had just been released; the tour had been set up by Mike Farrell from the William Morris Agency whose office was 37 floors up on Sixth Avenue – a great place to visit unless you were scared of heights.

Les lived at the bottom end of Fulham Road, in a two-bedroom flat by the river. One evening he was in the living room with his friends smoking an Arab shisha pipe filled with marijuana. In the bedroom was his mother who was staying with him at the time. She was suffering from depression and unbeknownst to Les, who was having a merry old time in the living room getting stoned and listening to loud music, his mum had taken an overdose of sleeping pills but having had a change of heart, decided to call an ambulance. So the doorbell rang, Les staggered to the front, opened up and was confronted by two ambulance men and two police officers. Of course he didn't know anything about what was going on in the bedroom and thought it was a bust!

Les's mother was swiftly treated by the paramedics with a stomach pump that saved her life. He, on the other hand, was immediately arrested owing to the all-pervasive clouds of aromatic smoke drifting from the living room. He was charged and remanded on bail and therefore was unable to fly out to work on what was Genesis's biggest US tour to date. The band were left with a choice: either get someone to do the lights who didn't know the music, or get someone who knows the music who could learn how to do the lights. They got in touch, asked if I would jump in and I said yes. Suddenly I was the official lighting guy.

Off we went a week later, travelling down the East Coast for a run of gigs. Mike Farrell had taken a bit of a punt and booked two shows way down south, one in Shreveport, Louisiana, and the other in Laurel, Mississippi, neither of which were exactly strongholds of the Genesis American fan club. We got as far as Memphis, where we went to visit Graceland, and received word that both gigs had been unceremoniously cancelled. A terrible disaster? I don't think so. I was with Mike, Tony and Margaret, in a shiny Chrysler Newport Custom rental car. We had lots of money and all we had to do was get ourselves within a week to Austin Texas where the band were booked to play at the Armadillo World Headquarters. Suddenly, to our great delight, we were on holiday. None of us had ever been to New Orleans so we drove down the Mississippi to the city they call 'The Big Easy,' booked into a hotel in the French Quarter, spent a couple of days soaking up the vibes in several jazz clubs, then drove round the Gulf of Mexico. On we went to Galveston and then up to Houston where we visited the Johnson Space Centre. Finally, we made our way to Austin, Phoenix and finished up in Los Angeles, quite a road trip for English folk from Surrey.

In Los Angeles we did a gig at the Santa Monica Civic Auditorium where all the important bands played in those days. Astonishingly, the *Cashbox* reviewer made special mention of my lights. It was gratifying to know that by now I'd got my act together with all the lighting cues. For the first time we hooked up with Dallas-based Showco who were providing all the sound and lighting equipment. Their lighting gofer on that tour was called Alan Owen who later became their top lighting guy. In 1987, backstage at Wembley, he told me that my light show had inspired him to become the best in the business. When Showco became massive, he developed the breakthrough technology called Varey lights for them.

Back in England, Les went to court, was fined and then jumped on a plane and arrived in California to take over from me. The last gig I did with the band was in San Francisco but while I was in LA I'd met a posh-spoken British guy called Tony Harrington who had been hired by Atlantic to be a liaison person, a good vibes guy for all the British groups on the label: Yes, Led Zeppelin and, by now, Genesis who had left Buddah and signed with Atlantic. Once again a crafty move orchestrated by Tony Smith.

So there I was in Los Angeles with my new pal Tony, all my wages, all my per diems, thousands of dollars and a ticket home to use when I wanted. It was the middle of 1974 and, at that time in LA, the music scene was brilliant. No prizes for guessing that I decided to stay.

Tony Harrington had a sister called Suzanne Maxwell who was divorced with three young children who were being looked after by her mother in Salem, Oregon. Meanwhile, Suzanne was living in LA in a house on Hemet Place, at the bottom of Laurel Canyon and I was invited to move in with her. She had a soft-top

Lincoln Continental that I was allowed to use, so there I was in California, footloose and fancy free with more than enough money to splash about. My friendship with Suzanne soon developed into something deeper and we spent four happy weeks hanging out together.

One trip I remember well from this period was when Tony and I went to Las Vegas to see Black Oak Arkansas, he as Atlantic's representative and me as a bystander keen to see this strange neon outpost in the Nevada desert. Black Oak was a heavy rock band from Arkansas with a very flamboyant singer who called himself Jim Dandy after a character in a 1956 R&B song about a ladykiller who rescues women from sticky situations and whom I knew of from the song 'Little Sister' by Elvis.

Tony had a room at the Holiday Inn and when we checked in my eyes were on stalks. There was no sign of reception. All you could see were slot machines stretching out to the horizon. The lobby was (no doubt still is) a gigantic casino. There are two things you need to know about hotels in Las Vegas. One, they don't have any windows so it's permanently night time. Two, they don't have clocks because they want you to forget what time it is. It's not called 'Lost Wages', as in the Steely Dan song, for nothing.

Jim Dandy had long, straight blonde hair halfway down his back and used to appear on stage topless; he had a good body and a hairy chest that he liked to set off against extremely tight blue and white striped trousers and knee-length tasselled boots, all impressively macho and about a million miles from my Genesis pals. Thus dressed, or not, he took the lift to the ground floor and snaked his way through all these people in the lobby, pulling away at their one-armed bandits accompanied by huge plastic cups full of money, dollar coins that you get as change in gas stations – but only in Nevada. They couldn't believe their eyes. Here, truly, was the splendour of Jim Dandy, rock's equivalent of a strutting peacock, making his way row upon row through middle-aged Middle Americans, no doubt God-fearing citizens with their blue rinses and synthetic pant-suits, throwing away their money with the abandon of lemmings leaping off a cliff.

Black Oak Arkansas had an extraordinary bus to alleviate the strain of touring. They were the first band that I'd ever come across who owned their own bus and what a bus it was. Country boys raised to prosper by the sweat of their brow, they could do their own carpentry and had fitted out their tour vehicle like a palace with bunks at the back and a communal area at the front. They had all mod-cons at their finger tips. Tony and I boarded this palace on wheels and cruised right down the Strip, past all the glittering Cathedrals of Saint Greed: The Sands, The Hilton and Caesars Palace. Up in lights were the names of the Gods appearing on their altars for a season: Elvis, Shirley Bassey, Tom Jones, and goodness knows who else. Then we arrived at the gig, a bog standard American basketball arena, and suddenly we weren't in Las Vegas any more. It was just like any other gig anywhere else in America with long-haired rock fans dressed in jeans and t-shirts, smoking joints and rooting for their bands by yelling 'boogie' at the tops of their voices. It was a big crowd because Black Oak were very popular in those days but their music wasn't my thing. We still had a blast and enjoyed, once again, the ride in our super bus back to the Holiday Inn where we found the blue rinse congregation still worshipping at the slot machines.

After a few weeks back in LA, Suzanne decided to pack up the house and move to Oregon to rejoin her mother and children. Perhaps this decision was not unrelated to the fact that her new housemate was a man of considerable experience when it came to moving stuff around in trucks. We packed up everything, loaded it into a U-Haul truck and prepared to drive to Oregon. Being a one-way truck rental and wanting to take her Lincoln with her, we needed to remove its drive shaft so that it could be attached to the back of the truck. This tricky bit of mechanical work was done by skilled workmen at the nearest garage and by the time we'd hooked it up behind the U-Hawl and were ready to go it was about five in the afternoon, far later than we'd intended. We had no other choice than to head straight out on to the freeway in the LA rush hour, bumper to bumper. For the first few miles I kept trying to shake off the Lincoln that was driving right up my backside!

With LA disappearing into the smog behind us, Suzanne and I headed on to US Route 1, up the California coast and certainly one of the most scenic drives in the world. On the first night we got as far as Morro Bay where we checked into separate rooms in a classic 1950s roadside motel. It was no fun negotiating the car park with this bloody great American car wedged up behind. Reversing was hell, to be avoided at all costs, but fortunately, there is a lot of space in America so you can usually make any manoeuvre you want in a forward gear. By the next night we reached Big Sur and beyond – all those places The Beach Boys liked to sing about in their paeans to California. In fact, we had reached Sausalito, just south of San Francisco. By this time, things had developed further between Suzanne and me so only one room was required.

The whole trip took about four days. We reached Salem, Oregon, disentangled the Lincoln and reunited Suzanne with her family. It was at this point that I knew I was falling for her. My dilemma was whether I really could become seriously involved with a woman some years older than me with three children to raise. I might have settled with her and be living now in Carmel, where she now lives, but my 22-year-old self decided that it was time to take my leave. It was a wrench. The sliding doors closed behind me and I headed north.

Greyhound buses and hitching were my preferred modes of transport. My route took me up through Northern Oregon and Washington State where I constantly marvelled at the vast expanse of wild nature. I went up to Seattle, then over the Cascade Mountains and up into the Canadian Rockies, skirting Vancouver until I reached Calgary where I met a Canadian guy from Ottawa who'd been skiing up in the Rockies. He'd spent all his money and needed a cheap way to get home. We decided to hitch together, right across Canada, a distance of over 2000 miles. After a while we found ourselves standing in pitch darkness in the pouring rain by the Trans Canadian highway. Eventually someone pulled up in a little English car, an Austin Allegro, so we piled in and he turned out to be a defiant Canadian redneck from Toronto who told us he was a truck driver. Why he was driving across Canada in a tiny car remained a mystery but he clearly had a bee in his bonnet about English automobiles. 'They're the best engineered cars in the world,' he kept telling us and we weren't about to argue.

The Trans Canadian Highway may sound very grand compared to the B743 but the reality is that for much of the way, it was no more than a two-lane road. This made it all the more alarming when our Allegro fan drove right over a dead cow lying across our path. I was amazed it didn't damage the car. My hitchhiking friend and I felt we should stop, pointing out that the animal might cause an accident, but our chauffeur was in no mood to consider other road users. 'No waaaaay, I ain't stopping,' he responded. We were now faced with the choice of losing our ride if we got out to move the cow in the pouring rain or staying put and leaving it in the road. Needless to say we stayed put.

Our driver was loquacious and we learned much about him, his family and where he lived in Toronto, which although tedious, would come in useful later. We got as far as the very west of the Great Lakes, a place called Thunder Bay on Lake Superior, where he suggested we stay in a motel while he stayed with a friend who lived nearby. He promised to pick us up in the morning but the morning came and went without any sign of him. He had dumped us in Thunder Bay. Unfortunately I'd left my camera in his car. It wasn't so much the camera that I regretted losing as the pictures I had taken to show friends back in the UK if and when I finally reached home. The two of us carried on hitching until we eventually decided to separate. I wanted to go to Toronto to get my camera back. He was heading home to Ottawa.

My last lift was in Sioux Saint Marie, famous for its nickel mines. The guy driving the van had been hang-gliding, not such a popular pastime as it is now. It's a tiring sport and he was totally exhausted. The only reason he had stopped to pick me was because he wanted me to drive. I duly got behind the wheel while he promptly fell asleep all the way to Toronto.

It was at this point that the seemingly irrelevant information that our Allegro fan had imparted became crucial to my needs, as did the map-reading skills I had acquired in the service of Genesis.

I was able to figure out from the phone book precisely where he lived, in a suburb of Toronto called Mississauga, and found my way to his house. Needless to say, he was astonished to see me on his doorstep – probably not too delighted either. He had given the camera to his son and thrown away the film. I got the camera back but I've never again felt an urge to drive an Allegro.

Next I headed further east to Ottawa, to stay with my hitching buddy who, like me, was still feeling a little guilty at leaving a dead cow in the road. His parents welcomed me to their French-speaking province where the Parliament building bears a striking resemblance to our own House of Commons beside the Thames. It is clearly a legacy of the Commonwealth era when architects saw no reason not to recreate a perfectly adequate centre of government.

My ultimate destination was in the very far east of Canada, north of the Saint Lawrence River. I was seeking out some people in the Gaspé Peninsula, a New Age Christian community, members of which I'd met at Findhorn and who had invited me to drop by if I was ever in the vicinity. At the time, of course, I never imagined this happening but here I suddenly was and I ended up staying with them. They were self-sufficient, very New Age and there was a lot of praying. They were very kind and welcoming to me and I was heartened by the way they created music with the local community. But…

Eventually I made my way back to Toronto and used my open ticket to fly home. I still had some money left and when I reached London I discovered that the band was working on what was to become *The Lamb Lies Down On Broadway*. However, more ominously, things in Camp Genesis were falling apart…

MY BOOK OF GENESIS

Chapter 12

WHY DID
PETER LEAVE GENESIS?

When I reached the farm in Wales
where they were recording The Lamb,
Jill described the situation as a nightmare.

It would probably be overstating the case, perhaps even a shade impertinent for me to suggest that my absence from the world of Genesis led to the instability that plagued them while I was larking about in North America, but it didn't take me long to deduce that all was not well with my old friends.

I settled back into my squat in Freston Road. My housemates had saved my room for me while I was away as I was still paying my £6 a week. In addition to the rent, this modest sum covered everything: rates, TV, phone and even the food that I hadn't consumed.

The first person I got in touch with was Mike Rutherford who informed me that Genesis were down in Wales making a new album, as yet untitled. They were living on a remote farm with a mobile recording studio and John Burns still behind the controls as producer. After recovering from jet lag, I clambered into my battered old green Ford Transit and paid them a visit. It was miles from nowhere, to quote Cat Stevens, but to understand why they weren't happy, we need to backtrack a bit.

Peter was the first member of Genesis to get married. He had taken the plunge with his longstanding girlfriend, Jill, whom he had known since our school days. They married in 1972 and because Jill's father happened to be Secretary to the Queen, the ceremony took place at St James's Palace. We all dressed up to the nines in hired kit, top hats and tails, the whole caboodle.

It followed that Peter and Jill were the first to have a child, a daughter they named Anna Marie. It was a very difficult birth and without exaggeration, touch and go for a while. To begin with, no one knew whether the baby would survive. Clearly this was an enormously stressful time for her parents. Anna Marie was only a few weeks old while they were recording the album that would eventually be called *The Lamb Lies Down On Broadway*. Not only were Peter and Jill new parents but they had just come through a terrifying ordeal. Anna cried a lot, no one was getting any sleep.

Meanwhile, the album was expanding and Peter was supposed to be writing the lyrics as it was his concept. The idea had come straight out of Peter's subconscious and was probably not the easiest to grasp insofar as the main character, a New York graffiti artist named Rael, undergoes a transformation akin to experiencing an acid trip, despite being written by someone who had never taken LSD in his life. Rael descends into an underworld and goes through an incredible journey of the soul, encountering a number of strange characters and bizarre creatures along the way.

So far so good but it was still a bit opaque. I remember that not long after it came out, I was staying with Peter at the cottage he had bought near Bath when his mother rang up. She had heard the album for the first time, read all the words and wanted to ask him about it. There he was on the phone for about 45 minutes trying to explain the symbolism to her. A lot of the album was about her, or at least about the way Peter had been brought up, and about sexual repression and the public schoolboy experiences. That was typical of Irene Gabriel. A lot of mums wouldn't have asked but she wanted to know precisely what Peter was getting at. I still don't know whether she was any the wiser at the end of their conversation.

Down in Wales I was excused my cooking duties because John Burns's wife was a dab hand in the kitchen and had taken on that role. It was a big house, easily able to accommodate everyone.

Margaret Banks and Angie Rutherford were also there, plus Steve's German wife Ellen with whom he later had a son they called Oliver. Only Phil was single though as the world knows, he would catch up in the marriage stakes in the fullness of time.

That was the scene in the Kingdom of Genesis which was now being disrupted by the dramatic shift in Peter's priorities on becoming a father. The others didn't quite understand what Peter was going through at the time; Tony Banks has since said since that he sympathises completely now with where Peter's head was at. Quite simply, Peter went through fatherhood a year or two before anyone else. You couldn't underestimate the effect this was going to have on the dynamics of the group.

Today, Phil Collins believes that too much pressure was placed on Peter, especially from Mike and Tony, although he admits that he, too, hadn't been aware of the full picture:

> *It was totally inappropriate behaviour to say you're in or you're out. But then we were all immature and nobody else had a family. So nobody knew those pressures, external domestic stuff. It was unfair. The band ought to have given him a bit more slack. I can understand why we didn't. With hindsight… now, three marriages and five kids later, I can understand it.*

> *… In certain respects Peter kept some of his cards close to his chest. I didn't know that Jill was having a difficult pregnancy. I wasn't privy to that conversation. I guess it must have been Tony and Mike, the royal we, that in the end decided on the in or out. I don't remember having that conversation with them.*

> *… It was clumsy, and probably meant to jolt him. I think it was kind of a rank thing, pulling rank. Probably at that point there was a lot of peacocking going around. So that probably had something to do with it.*

Tony Banks, normally a sea of calm when things became frantic, can also recall the impending crisis:

When Peter said he was going to leave, we had one very fraught day thinking what we might do, and then Strat showed up and persuaded Peter to stay. William Friedkin had seen a short piece Peter had written on the cover of the live album and wanted Pete to break up the band in order for them to write a script together. But Peter felt he'd had enough. I don't remember him talking about leaving again while we were actually recording The Lamb. *For me, it wasn't a very happy time for all sorts of other reasons. I enjoyed that album the least of all the albums we've ever done. I didn't enjoy the tour either because I knew that Peter was going to leave.*

The highpoint of *The Lamb* for Tony was 'Fly On a Windshield':

That's my favourite moment, when that bang comes in, maybe the best moment of Genesis.

Genesis had always been a very democratic outfit. When there was a decision to be made Tony Smith would come down and there'd be a war cabinet. Decisions were taken on a majority vote. If the issue on the table was whether or not they were going to tour America for three months in a bid to crack the US once and for all, then it would be four votes in favour and one against. Of course Peter would always be the one. He was constantly being dragged in a direction in which he didn't want to go – or so it seemed to him at the time.

When I reached the farm in Wales where they were recording *The Lamb*, Jill described the situation as a nightmare. Leaving was certainly on Peter's mind but he had yet to make a final decision. At this stage, he had only discussed it with Jill. I could see that a tremendously stressful scenario was building up, not just over Peter's family situation but also because of the length of the album, which had expanded into a double. This of course meant even more work for him; Peter writes fantastic lyrics but they don't come easily. At any given moment he's probably got 35 songs all mapped out, possibly even in demo form and recorded, but he'll have lyrics for only one of them, or maybe two at a pinch.

A famous story emerged much later in Peter's career when he was in the studio with the French Canadian producer, Daniel Lanois. Lanois was getting so frustrated with the lack of lyrical progress that he trapped Peter in the studio, nailed a plank of wood over the door and didn't let him out until he'd completed the song.

From the very beginning, Peter had always been the main lyricist in Genesis, although from necessity the others would blossom into writing lyrics much later. *The Lamb* was Peter's concept and, to be honest, I don't think the others had any idea what the hell it was all about – some crazy story about spray guns and a lamb descending into the bowels of Manhattan – but it didn't matter. What was important was that the whole thing was late, delayed because it had turned into a double album and because Peter could not be rushed into meeting his own high standard of lyric writing.

The American tour had been booked and the dates couldn't be changed, so in the end they actually did the worst possible thing you can do, which is to go on the road playing new music that no one has heard before. Not only that but they were presenting a huge concept affair, playing it from start to finish, including unbelievable sets and costumes. The fans hadn't heard a note of it before so, even for the most faithful Genesis followers, it was tough to digest. From the record company's point of view it was madness, not least because the record wasn't even in the shops, so even if the fans did like it, they wouldn't be able to get hold of a copy.

The US tour started in October and the record was released in November. 'What on earth is going on?' was the response from American audiences – or so I heard. They had a complicated back projection, one of the first bands to do so, and it was all very long winded. Then, after it was all over and everyone was left scratching their heads, they came back and did 'The Return Of the Giant Hogweed', which everyone would have recognised. 'Thank God, something we know,' was the palpable reaction.

America was certainly a real struggle but I wasn't tour managing anymore. That job had been taken up by Regis Boff. I decided to join the tour in Europe, but more as a friend than an employee. For all the problems, I still think it was an amazing show. Tony Banks said it really only worked fully on two occasions but I don't think it was quite as bad as that. The back projection was very primitive compared to today: three Kodak Carousel slide projectors on stepladders, all connected up so that when the slide changed it was all one huge panoramic shot of New York. It was brilliant. There's a Canadian Genesis tribute band called 'The Musical Box' and many years later the band gave them the slides so they could recreate the show.

Before they finished the American tour, Peter announced he was going to leave, telling the band but not the press. Tony remembers it only too well:

> Peter left in the middle of the tour, in Cleveland in that terrible hotel, Swingos. That was when he finally said he was definitely going to leave and then we had to carry on with the rest of the tour knowing that.

Steve Hackett tried to talk Peter out of his decision:

> I couldn't quite believe that he was going to do the tour and do so many gigs, nine months on the road, and then leave the band. I loved Pete. I struggled with The Lamb Lies Down On Broadway because I knew that he had a single-minded vision at that point and he was going to be as bloody-minded as anyone else. But when the irresistible force meets the immovable object and you've got two of them in a band together, sparks are going to fly and it's not necessarily going to serve the best interests of the music, so I think that Pete and Tony were on a terrible collision course there. Tony was going to fill the album up with as many notes as possible and Pete was going to fill it up with as many lyrics as possible and the rest of us were just watching this thinking, 'I'd better make a noise.' Having said that, there's not an album on the planet like it.

I knew what was happening, of course, and it wasn't comfortable. The last gig Peter did with the band was at Besançon in France, a town that features later in this story. So that was it. He quit and moved down to Woolly Mill, a cottage in a tiny village outside Bath. Having been brought up on a farm in Surrey, Peter had always wanted to live in the country and settled there as soon as he could. He devoted himself to his young family, to growing vegetables and exploring his own spirituality. He even considered joining a commune, an interest we shared. During this period Peter was involved in a programme called Silva Mind Control, invented by an American, Jose Silva, a course that he attended with my friend Betsy Gibson, Simon Cowe's wife.

It was around this time that I decided to sign up for the EST (Erhard Seminars Training). Founded by American Werner Erhard in California in 1971, it was part of the Human Potential Movement of the 1960s and 70s. The stated purpose of the course was to 'transform your experience of living so that the situations you had been trying to change, or were putting up with, clear up just in the process of life itself'. The EST training was a very creative and dramatic affair. I had experienced encounter groups and other similar workshops before but this was something totally different. I attended with Janessa, my girlfriend, and Peter and Jill Gabriel. I didn't know it at the time but the course was exactly what I needed at that moment in my life. It completely shook me up, opening doors to new ways of being. EST focused on the ideas of accountability, possibilities and at its heart, taking personal responsibility for your life. I learned an enormous amount from it and nearly 40 years later, I still feel many of the benefits that I gained.

While Peter was enjoying the bucolic life, the Genesis machine rolled on and they started writing material for *Trick Of the Tail*, the first album without Peter, which would be released in February 1976. The press were informed, and in their edition of August 16th 1975, *Melody Maker* emblazoned on its front page, 'GABRIEL OUT OF GENESIS', with a picture of Peter in his batwings costume.

The cat was out of the bag and word got out that Genesis needed a new singer so they started auditions. To my astonishment, Mike Rutherford actually said to me, 'You're in the frame', but I never heard any more about it. Either way, I'm not sure whether I would have accepted it even if the role had been offered.

Try as they might – and they tried quite a number – Genesis just couldn't find anyone to fit the bill. The auditions were held in the Una Billings studio opposite The Richmond pub in Shepherd's Bush where they had written 'Supper's Ready' and some of those who tried out have since become big names. One was Graham Bonnet who went on to sing with Rainbow, on their hit 'Since You've Been Gone'. The problem was that Peter's shoes were very difficult to fill and in the meantime they'd written all the songs for the new album and had started recording the backing tracks with Phil doing guide vocals. Then of course, the inevitable happened.

It was a gradual thing really, everyone coming to the same conclusion. 'We can't find a singer,' they moaned. Then it became, 'Well, bloody hell, we've got one already. Why are we bothering?' So Phil took over and at first faced a barrage of criticism for sounding like Peter. What people never fully understood was that they always sang together. Phil often sang in unison with Peter while playing the drums, so when people said, 'Oh, he sounds just like Peter Gabriel' he didn't actually. He sounded just like himself.

Phil was definitely the stronger singer out of the rest of them. With the best will in the world Mike and Tony are not singers. They could do backing vocals but they would never have set the world alight. It was Phil or no one. Also, there was never any real thought about calling it a day when Peter left. When people asked how they could continue without him, this simply spurred them on. They dug their heels in and said, 'Fuck it, we'll show them.' Much later, when interviewed in America, they were asked why they carried on and admitted it was because they were so bloody minded. As for me, it felt like a different situation than when Anthony Philips left all those years ago. I wasn't so sure that they should carry on and even remember going down to Tony and Margaret's house in Twickenham and telling him that it might be time to close Genesis down.

Tony wasn't having it. He might be the quiet one in the band but when he sets his mind on something he won't let go, and when it comes to bloody mindedness he takes the gold, even more so than Peter who'd have run him a close race for the silver. In that same

American interview, the guy asking the questions was trying to make some point about how Genesis were unique in the whole of rock by managing to replace a front man as successfully as they did. This stuck in Tony's mind as not being quite right. The interviewer was trying to move things along but Tony wouldn't have it. 'AC/DC did quite well on that,' he says, and starts citing all these bands that have replaced their singer. He's totally undermining this guy who gets quite pissed off. At one point the interviewer says something like, 'You have to agree with me on this,' and this was like a red rag to a bull with Tony Banks. No, he certainly would not agree with him on this. When the interview finally appears to be moving on, you can see Tony's brain churning away and he says, 'Fleetwood Mac'. He just wouldn't let go. It was brilliant. Game, set and match to Tony. That's his personality in a nutshell.

Of course, the record labels were extremely worried about Peter's departure. Record labels don't like change; they like everything to stay the same as if they were selling detergent or breakfast cereals, but they needn't have worried. *Trick Of the Tail* was a huge success and as we also know, Genesis with Phil Collins up front were even more popular.

Nevertheless, they were all quite nervous about going back on the road without Peter. When Phil eventually agreed to become the lead singer, he told everyone that he couldn't bear the idea of being like Chris Curtis of The Searchers or Mickey Dolenz of The Monkees; in other words, being a lead singer who sings from behind the drums. He'd always thought it looked really naff; if he was going to be the front man, they would have to get another drummer for the road. One of Phil's favourite drummers was Bill Bruford who had started out in Yes but left them to form a jazz group with a keyboard player called Dave Stewart (not the guy from Eurythmics but from Hatfield & The North). Bill was happy to join and with his astonishing technique and creativity, he made a great addition to the band. For the record, Bill is the only musician to have played in Yes, Genesis and King Crimson.

While all this was going on, I went back to being a removals man for Gentle Ghost. I was surprised when out of the blue,

Tony Smith phoned to ask if I fancied doing the first leg of the European tour. They seemed to want the reassurance of me being around, so there I was again, tour manager of Genesis in the summer of 1976, that famously hot, dry period when it didn't rain from May until the August Bank holiday. The rain finally came in the middle of the Notting Hill Carnival!

I can still remember it being so hot under the lights at these big venues that we had to give the band salt tablets because they were sweating so much. The first rehearsals with Phil were held at Shepperton Studios. By then they each had their own technical roadies for their guitars and keyboards and the Showco crew came over from Texas to handle the tour. Their lighting guy, Alan Owen, brought me a 'summer straw', which is what they call those huge Texan hats – straw for summer, felt for winter.

The London gigs were at the Hammersmith Odeon. One funny moment stands out for me. I was sitting in the audience with Tony Smith and they were rehearsing 'Supper's Ready' with Phil up on a riser at the back. He was about to sing one of the big climactic verses when they overdid the smoke; he disappeared completely in a white cloud and bravely kept on singing, coughing and spluttering all the while. Tony and I nearly wet ourselves laughing.

The set they played was mostly from *Trick Of the Tail* plus what might be called their greatest hits, including 'Supper's Ready'. Genesis didn't play songs from *The Lamb* until later, probably because it was Peter's baby. It was thought that cutting down on songs that were particularly associated with Peter would make it less likely that fans and/or critics would make comparisons.

As I have said, Phil took to his new role really well. He had been a child actor and he soon developed his own stage shtick. Peter used to tell his long stories but Phil wasn't inclined to copy that. Instead, he developed the character of a song and dance man with his tambourine, bish bash bosh on his knees and sides and head, an unusual front man for the era but totally original in his own way, just as Peter was in *his* way. Phil was never going to be one of those macho guys with skin tight jeans and a bare chest like Robert Plant or Roger Daltrey or indeed Jim Dandy, so he became a cheeky chappie. This didn't stop him from having his fair share of female admirers. Not all girls wanted a strutting sex symbol, it seemed.

From that point on, Genesis fans split into two groups: the real diehards who loved Genesis up to *The Lamb* and the ones who preferred the post-*Lamb*/Peter era. But now this second lot were beginning to outnumber the original fans. People loved the shows with Phil and they showed up in their thousands.

I was back on the payroll for three months, having briefing meetings with Tony Smith, going through details and logistics. By this time we had a travel agent and once I knew the tour dates, we would figure out how many people were in the entourage and what we needed for transport and accommodation: a bus for the crew, airline tickets, cars, how many hotel rooms, etc. There were more than 30 people on the road with us by now, the lighting was bigger and better, the PA more powerful. It was mostly rented from Showco and when the tour finished it all went back on the plane to Dallas. Our stage equipment, the gear that Genesis actually owned, was stored in Shepperton, until they found a place in Chiddingfold, Surrey, called Fisher Lane Farm, where they eventually built their own studio.

I didn't do the American tour. Instead, I went back to my squat in Freston Road and waited for a call. There was a sleeping giant down there near Bath, not far from a place they called Solsbury Hill and I knew that sooner or later, he'd wake up and roar.

MY BOOK OF GENESIS

Chapter 13

THE KRAKEN WAKES

In my view, Peter was, and remains,
one of the most disciplined rock stars in the business
with a world view that cares more for the
common good than material gain.

For the best part of a year Peter Gabriel meditated on the meaning of existence, sampled the delights of his own vegetable garden and doted on his infant daughter, soon to be joined by a sister, Melanie, but he was no more likely to abandon music that I was to join a monastery. Inevitably, he'd been tinkering around on the piano and writing songs. One of the first came about because he lived near Solsbury Hill, a small flat-topped mound above his village from where he could look down on the Roman city of Bath.

Peter liked to go running up on the hill, hence the lyrics: 'Climbing up on Solsbury Hill, I can see the city lights' but the song is really about him leaving Genesis, as in the line: 'I walked right out of the machinery, my heart going boom, boom, boom.' Two extremely powerful songs emerged during his sabbatical, the other being 'Here Comes the Flood', a tremendous number that Robert Fripp later covered on his solo album *Indiscipline*.

There was never any doubt that Peter would continue as a musician, but from now onwards it would be on his own terms. Tony Smith was still managing him and he was still signed to

Charisma and Atlantic (actually their Atco subsidiary) in America. It was just a matter of waiting for a different set of machinery to start turning again.

Peter decided to record his first solo album in Toronto in early 1976 with Bob Ezrin as the producer. He was determined to create something that sounded nothing like Genesis and one way of succeeding in this was to make it an all American affair. To this end, Peter allowed Bob Ezrin to select the backing musicians. Ezrin put together a crew that included Steve Hunter, a guitarist who played with Alice Cooper and whose albums he'd produced, and Alan Schwartzberg on drums. Alan suggested Tony Levin on bass because they'd done sessions together, part of a team of musicians in New York who were the kings of studio work at the time. In those days they'd arrive at the studio and find bits of paper stuck to a noticeboard saying, 'Tony Levin call... such and such a number', for the next session. They had played on dozens of jingles together, bread and butter work as we might call it in the UK but the staff of life for working professionals like Alan and Tony. I'm sure Tony is deeply grateful to Alan for suggesting him for Peter's album because this subsequently turned into a large portion of his eminent career. This included meeting Robert Fripp and eventually becoming a fixture in King Crimson.

Robert Fripp, he of the national health spectacles and profoundly analytical mind, was the only British player on Peter's new album. There was a percussionist called Jimmy Maelen and Larry Fast, a synthesiser player who had a band called Synergy that Peter admired a lot. The two guitar players, Fripp and Hunter, were totally different in their styles, Hunter picking out the acoustic guitar intro to 'Solsbury Hill' that we all know and love. It was and remains a striking introduction to Peter's solo career, in many ways responsible for his debut album's No.7 place in the UK charts and No.38 in America.

Recorded between July 1976 and January 1977, with additional sessions at Olympic and Morgan in London, it was released in the following March. Although I didn't become involved with Peter again until after the album was recorded, he and I were in regular touch as friends. It was only a matter of time before our conversations turned to when he would tour again and, now free of Genesis, I offered my services. Peter said it would be great to have me along, so I dusted off my briefcase and off we went. My living circumstances hadn't changed much in all this time so a few weeks on the road with my old friend seemed like a good idea.

We'll leave Peter and his boom-boom-booming heart in Somerset for a moment while I digress into domestic matters.

I was still humping furniture for people on the move and bedding down in the squat on Freston Road, but things were coming to a head there with the London County Council (the LCC) breathing down our necks. Once a housing authority with estates of houses built under its leader, Horace Cutler, all over Greater London and even some further afield, they had decided to get out of being landlords and bequeath the housing stock to whichever local authority the homes fell in.

One problem for the LCC was that many of the properties they were about to hand over were empty. Another was squatters like us. So it was that someone came up with the brilliant idea of solving both problems at a stroke by asking the squatters to move into the empty properties before the buildings were handed over to the local authority. This was called the Squatters Amnesty and under it we received letters from the LCC (later the GLC under Ken Livingstone) explaining that we had to register by a certain date in order to be offered a council property. We would be given a proper tenancy, nothing temporary, which was a rare thing to have and quite valuable in terms of security. It was a once and once only offer that we had to accept without delay or the deal was off. Of course we wanted in.

The snag, as far as we were concerned, was that we were squatting two houses knocked together, with seven or eight of us in residence, and of course, they didn't have anything big enough to offer us when we registered as a group. They tried though. We were offered a property in a place called South Oxhey, on the tube line out towards Watford somewhere. When we went to see this house it was on an absolutely God-awful sink estate and had only four bedrooms. We went back to them and said thanks very much but the property is unsuitable. So nothing happened and we split up. Some of our number accepted tenancies elsewhere and out of the blue, three of us, which just happened to be me and my girlfriend Janessa and another girl called Cass Ingerson, were offered a three-bedroom flat at the top of Trellick Tower, a famous building next to the Westway. Trellick is an imposing skyscraper (by British standards) with a separate stack for the lifts and bridges connecting to the main building. It was Grade II listed, designed by the Hungarian-born architect Ernö Goldfinger who among other things was responsible for the debacle that is the Elephant & Castle, exemplifying an architectural movement from the 60s that became known as New Brutalism.

Whenever I used to tell people that Goldfinger designed Trellick Tower they would often wonder whether there was any connection between the architect and Ian Fleming's arch villain. There is a story, perhaps apocryphal, that does link them. Goldfinger bought a plot of land on Willow Road overlooking Hampstead Heath and applied for planning permission to build a row of three houses – a large one in the middle for him and two smaller ones on either side that he could sell off to fund the whole project. He wanted to use the same building technique as had been used for Trellick and not unnaturally, the good people of Hampstead took strong offence to this and fought tooth and nail with the Camden planning department, lobbying for permission to be refused. Eventually permission *was* granted and he built the houses. One of those living nearby who objected very strongly was Ian Fleming's mother, who at the time he was writing that particular Bond adventure used to ring her son and complain, 'That bastard Goldfinger. He's going to get away with building these horrible houses in our road.' So it is said, that's how Fleming came to give the name Goldfinger to his notorious baddie.

Back at Trellick, our flat was on the 27th floor on the end of the building, with a huge south-facing picture window and balcony that overlooked the canal and the railway lines into Paddington. On the end facing east were two medium-sized bedrooms and then a larger bedroom looking out north towards Hampstead and Highgate – stunning views from a very well constructed building, solid as a rock and with heating and lifts that worked efficiently enough. This represented a penthouse lifestyle that any New Yorker would have lusted after but it was a bit novel for most Londoners at the time.

Of course we took it. It was inexpensive, we were three young people, all in work and in no time we did the place up. I was living at Trellick when I began working again with Peter and it wasn't long before I realised that his idiosyncratic ways hadn't changed much since the days when he wore a red dress and a fox's head.

This much was evident when he got a bee in his bonnet about not wanting to give his new album a title. It was to be called *Peter Gabriel*, just Peter Gabriel, and I believe he thought of it as being like an upmarket magazine, with only a title and the same for every issue. Now there is nothing unusual with singer songwriters naming their first album after themselves – many of them have done so over the years – but when it came to the second album being called simply *Peter Gabriel*, and the same with the third, you can see where confusion might occur. If ever there was a metaphor for the way Peter acts, or declines to act, it is here in a nutshell. Decisions would have to be made but Peter would prevaricate, eternally refusing to make up his mind; quite often this would go on for so long that when it came to crunch time, no decision was ever made because the window of opportunity had closed. The result was that Peter robbed himself of the possibility in order to put his point of view across. And that's exactly what happened with his first three albums.

Those of you who have read this book so far might be wondering why, if Peter spent time on courses designed to improve mind control, he wasn't more resolute in such matters, but the fact is the courses didn't make him particularly decisive. He might disagree but it is an interesting dichotomy that makes him in part the artist that he is. We can be thankful that his fastidious nature, even if it did cause innumerable delays, has produced such a wonderful body of work.

With regard to the album titles, what happened of course was that in the fullness of time the world named them for him based on the covers: the first is now referred to as 'Car', the second 'Scratches' and the third 'Melt', a technique involving a Polaroid photo that was rubbed with a coin to make Peter's face resemble molten wax dripping from a candle.

The touring started in early 1977 with numerous shows in America followed by more in Europe. I acted as tour manager, overseeing a crew from Showco alongside the beginnings of a regular team of roadies that Peter and Tony Smith had recruited. A couple of guys came over from Genesis, the usual suspects in many ways, so in this regard there was an unbroken thread from the original gang. Peter performed in halls that held five to six thousand fans, some European venues even larger, demonstrating that he was already at a certain level of fame. It was a well-oiled machine, rock having evolved to a degree of professionalism and sophistication undreamt of in the days when we all piled into a Ford Transit along with all the gear.

If the support team had a whiff of the past about it, the show certainly didn't. 'That was then and this is now,' was very much Peter's attitude and thankfully the audiences accepted it. 'This is the new stuff,' he seemed to be saying. The set he played consisted entirely of songs from the new album with the occasional cover version thrown in for good measure, among them a cracking rendering of Marvin Gaye's 'Ain't That Peculiar'. He wore a grey tracksuit, no fancy costumes, no fancy lights, all very straightforward. It looked and sounded nothing like Genesis. Although in time the shows would become more elaborate in terms of visuals and the manner in which he performed, he played that first tour absolutely straight. It was quite brave of him really, like when Paul McCartney first toured as himself in the 70s without so much as a hint of a Beatles song.

In many ways the job of tour managing Peter ought to have been easier after all my experience with Genesis, but the truth is that he became more and more demanding as time went on. Just as exasperating for everyone was the vacillation that was part of Peter's character. We'd have people asking us to do things, making offers, and Peter wouldn't say yes and he wouldn't say no. Quite often the scenario would be that he would prevaricate for so long that the offer was abandoned and I was constantly in the middle, charged with talking to Peter about this and that but being deferred again and again. It used to drive his manager, Tony Smith, crazy. I have to say that more often than not, I felt that it acted to Peter's detriment though he probably wouldn't agree.

There is no question that Peter is difficult to work with as, of course, are many great performers – or so I've heard. I can remember the first inklings I had that I was going to be faced with a choice: whether to stay friends with Peter *or* keep working for him, the two being largely irreconcilable. More and more I was coming to realise that the time would arrive when I would have to opt for one or the other.

Whether this had anything to do with Tony Smith handing over Peter's management to Gail Colson after the first album was released is not for me to say. This happened while they were recording the second album, Gail having quit as general manager of Charisma to join Hit & Run, Tony Smith's management company. Of more import was the fact that Genesis was becoming enormous and managing them alone was a full-time job for Tony.

It's important also to remember that Peter was on his own now. Having been one of five, with responsibilities split among them, the buck stopped with him, which put him under greater pressure and probably made him more exacting. He was evolving as a solo artist, developing his myriad interests and had fingers in a gazillion different pies. It's not an easy life being a rock performer at the highest level, a level that Peter certainly sought to attain. While fans might envy what appears to them to be a life of riches, mansions, expensive cars and the adoration of millions, with millions in the bank, the reality of Peter's chosen lifestyle couldn't have been more different. In my view, Peter Gabriel was, and remains, among the most disciplined rock stars in the business with a world view that cares more for the common good than material gain.

Out on the road, after the years with Genesis I found it fascinating to be surrounded mainly by Americans. They were all impressively experienced musicians. Steve Hunter, the guitarist who had toured with Alice Cooper, was incredibly funny, a brilliant mimic who kept us in stitches with his endless repertoire of accents. I became particularly close to Tony Levin and his wife Teri, staying with them at their home in Woodstock after the tour, later enjoying a canal trip with them in the south of France, joined by my girlfriend Janessa.

When the tour was over, I was retained by Peter as what was known in the trade as his 'perse' (personal manager) and we moved on to the next phase of his career, the writing and recording of his second album, the one that became known as 'Scratches'. At the time there was a tax advantage to recording outside of the UK. Accordingly, we went to a studio in the southern Netherlands in a town called Hilvarenbeek. Peter made the unusual choice of inviting Robert Fripp to produce the record.

Before leaving for the Netherlands, Peter held a series of rehearsals at a country house hotel called Watley Manor near Tetbury in Gloucestershire. It suited him to be able to rehearse close to family and home in Bath. A few new musicians were needed and he began by recruiting a percussionist named Maruga, a wonderfully crazy guy from Detroit and one of a series of strange types that Peter was always hearing about somehow. Maruga had an extraordinary kit with plastic bleach bottles that were filled with rocks and beads. In spite of his exotic sounds, he didn't work out and was sent home. Peter also decided to hire another keyboard player, again a guy who used only one name. His US passport named him as Todd Cochran but he was known as Bayeté, one of the more pretentious names I encountered. He turned out to be a really difficult character, leading me to conclude that deep insecurities in one of the musicians tend to lead to issues on tour.

To all intents and purposes, apart from Tony Levin on bass and Larry Fast on synths, this was a new band. Peter brought in Sid McGinnis on guitar and a drummer called Jerry Marotta, brother of Rick who had been his first choice but turned out to be too busy. We all, including Fripp, ensconced ourselves in Watley Manor, the Americans thrilled to be staying in an actual English manor house with the added bonus of an excellent restaurant. This was the period when Fripp was working with David Bowie and he was often on the phone to him in Berlin where Bowie was working on his *Heroes* album. They would have recorded the song 'Heroes', some might say Bowie's greatest work, around this time too. (On their most recent tour, as a tribute to Bowie, King Crimson played 'Heroes' as their second encore with Fripp replicating that famously dense guitar part he laid down for the song.)

I remember going to Heathrow to pick up the American musicians and an announcement came over the tannoy, 'Will the person meeting Jerome David Marotta please make their way to the meeting place,' and there was Jerry. Jerome indeed. He'd been in a band called Orleans who had a hit with the song 'Dance With Me', and had become infamous for having one of the most embarrassing album covers ever. The band, including Jerry, were photographed in the nude. He has never lived it down. My first impression of him was of a warm hearted, playful and very smart guy. I fell in love with Jerry in an instant and we've been good friends ever since.

We all moved over to the Netherlands for the recording and spent the next several weeks living there. Peter and Robert wanted to experiment with setting up as if the band were playing live, with all the gear in one studio. They played loud, all of them really live and alive, instead of the usual overdubbing studio set-up. It was a good idea to try but it didn't really work. The band ended up building up the sound in a more conventional way. As ever, we needed to arrange accommodation for everyone. We found a big house for us all to share but Robert preferred to be on his own in a nearby hotel. I remember one day driving over to the hotel to pick him up to take him to the studio. I called from the lobby and he said, 'Come up, I'm not quite ready.' When I got to his room, he was practising his guitar and pointed to a chair. I sat down and he proceeded to play to me for about 10 minutes. Just me! What a privilege. (At the time of writing [August 2016], my wife Maggie and I were very fortunate to be invited to a post-rehearsal run through of King Crimson gearing up for their Autumn European tour. After the show Maggie and I were chatting to Robert and she asked him what he was going to do that evening. He said, 'I'll be going to my hotel room to practise my guitar'. *Plus ça change.*)

The recording lasted until Christmas 1977 when everyone went home for a break before the New York phase, which began in January at the Hit Factory in Manhattan. This was the era of Freddie Laker and his Skytrain, so flying to and from New York was cheap and easy. Peter was installed in a hotel called the Americana City Squire (now the Red Coach Inn), just north of Times Square on Seventh Avenue. He liked to stay there because on the top floor there was an indoor swimming pool for his much loved and needed early morning swim. Conveniently, the Hit Factory was only about five blocks away. We all stayed at the Americana apart from Jerry who was living in his brother Rick's apartment just near where the midtown tunnel crosses under the East River and connects with Queens.

Early in the year Peter asked me to fly back to the UK and collect Jill and their two little girls, along with Jill's sister Sally. He longed to have them with him in New York. We flew Pan Am and because it was the winter and no one was flying, the tickets were dirt cheap. On arriving back on the East Coast we flew straight into a terrible snowstorm, a complete whiteout, and along with nine other jumbo jets bound for New York, were diverted down to Washington DC. It was lucky we had the girls with us; we were able to play the 'small-children-in-distress' card with the result that we were bussed out to a place called Leesburg in Virginia, an hour away, to a hotel in the middle of nowhere. They gave us rooms, fed us and we fell into bed exhausted. We woke in the morning to blazing sunshine reflected off the snow like Showco's finest white Super Trooper stage lights. I trekked across a field knee-deep in snow and hitched a ride into Leesburg where I managed to find a car rental office that was actually open. I hired the only car available: a Ford Thunderbird.

When I drove back to our motel to pick up my precious charges, Sally opened her hotel room door and yelled 'It's an American car!' She was thrilled.

In the 1970s the typical family car in America was vast. Gas was cheap and this beast was no exception. In spite of being only a few feet shorter than a London bus, space inside the car and boot was strangely limited. We only just managed to cram ourselves in with all the luggage. By now the roads were opening up and we were able to drive all the way to the city up Interstate 95. When we arrived everything was shut down because of the snow and I was the hero of the hour for getting the family safely there, albeit a day late. All in a day's work for a perse.

The snow in New York was particularly bad that winter, or good, depending on your point of view. It can be very beautiful, pure white, at least for the first 24 hours. Then they plough the streets and huge banks of snow pile up by the sidewalks. You have to clamber over them somehow and there are puddles that may or may not be frozen. You don't know until you step in them and if they're not frozen you're in icy water up to your kneecaps. We all bought these big clumpy rubber galoshes from a hardware store and trudged to the studio looking like anglers by some Scottish loch.

Peter's family loved their stay in New York that winter. None of them had ever seen snow like this, so it was a pity that they'd already returned home when another downfall, even bigger than the first, landed on the city. It was evening and we were all in the Ziegfeld cinema on 55th Street watching *Close Encounters Of the Third Kind*, which had just been released. It was snowing when we went in at about five o'clock and still snowing when we came out almost two-and-a-half hours later. It just kept on coming down through the night until 15 or 16 inches had piled up in the streets. The English may be accused of talking too much about the weather but for a young Englishman this was a weather event worth talking about.

We woke up in the morning to no traffic. Outside our hotel window people were skiing down Seventh Avenue. Long Island was completely closed down. Because the Hit Factory was near our hotel, our work wasn't affected since we could traipse to the studio in our beloved galoshes. The whole world was at a stop but we kept going. In the years since then, I've experienced countless major snowstorms all over America and they have always thrilled me.

When the album was finished, the graphic designer Storm Thorgerson from Hipgnosis (the man who designed the famous cover for Pink Floyd's *Dark Side Of the Moon*) came up with various concepts for the album cover. He arrived with three or four ideas to show us; Peter decided on the 'scratches' concept and off we went down to the lower West Side to have the photographs taken. A year later 10cc had an album out and went for one of the other designs that Storm had shown us. That could have been Peter's, I thought when I saw it in a record shop.

Chapter 14

BUSTED IN ST GALLEN

I realised how catastrophically careless I had been –
I had left my briefcase full of drugs in the lobby
of the Rotterdam Hilton!

When singers or instrumentalists leave established groups their subsequent records are invariably referred to as solo albums. Sooner or later the prefix 'solo' is dropped and the shorter the length of time it takes for this to occur is surely a measure of the success of the artists' solo career. In Peter's case it didn't take long at all, perhaps helped by his decision to call the first three albums simply *Peter Gabriel*, but I believe there was more to it than that. His determination to make a clean break from Genesis, his style of presentation on stage and the nature of the music he produced all hastened the perception that Peter Gabriel was *Peter Gabriel*, not a *solo* singer, whatever that means, and certainly not someone who was hanging on to the coat tails of his former group.

By the spring of 1978, his second album was complete and we were gearing up for another round of touring. In time, this routine of write, rehearse, record and tour would become tiresome for Peter but in the age before videos, not to mention MTV and the internet, it was what you had to do to sell your record. He was well aware of this.

Peter's band had by now become a fixture: Tony Levin on bass, Larry Fast on synths, Sid McGinnis on guitar and Jerry Marotta on drums. They were a well-drilled crew. We went out on the road late that summer with an extended set that incorporated songs from both of Peter's albums, among them a blues number from 'Car' called 'Waiting For the Big One' on which Peter performed a stunt that in many ways epitomised the inventiveness he brought and would continue to bring to his stage shows.

'Big One' featured a long blues guitar solo in the middle, after the second chorus. During it Peter would come off stage, disappear for a few minutes and reappear somewhere in the theatre, usually on the balcony. He and I would have prearranged the whole stunt. I'd meet him in the wings, we'd go out of the stage door, walk up the side of the theatre, re-enter at the front where a guy who worked for the promoter would be ready at the doors to let us in and then Peter would go up the stairs to the balcony. The verse would start again and off he'd go, singing into a radio mic. The spotlights would pick him up unexpectedly, somewhere in the audience, and the fans loved it.

It was all Peter's idea. He was always very imaginative, forever looking for ways to be different, to do something dramatic that audiences wouldn't be expecting. By now he had graduated from the grey tracksuit into a pair of leather trousers and one of those white judo tops that made him stand out in the spotlights. So he'd be up there with the audience going nuts and before they had quite realised what was going on, we would have scooted back downstairs where the spots would pick him up again; he'd make his way down the aisle, still singing; the closer we got to the stage the greater the rough and tumble as fans got out of their seats to touch him. I was right next to him throughout all of this and we'd usually get a couple of the promoter's guys and two of our own crew who would make their way towards us, so there would be four or five of us close at hand to protect him. No one would want to hurt Peter, they were just fans getting a bit over enthusiastic, but the judo shirt was usually ripped open before we could hoist him up on to the stage. A huge cheer would go up and then we'd disappear. It was a great stunt and although others tried something similar, Peter was definitely the first to dream up this way of making closer contact with his audience.

I always thought it was especially brave of Peter considering that all those years ago, at Aylesbury, he had made the mistake of jumping feet first into a crowd that backed away, breaking his ankle as a result. It made him realise that he needed to fall back flat, and later, when he sang a song called 'Lay Your Hands On Me', he would stand at the front and drop himself backwards, trusting his fans to catch him. It was the most unbelievable thing to do, especially for someone who had previously injured himself, but he did it and they would lovingly pass him around. Many rock stars pay lip service to the idea of 'getting down with the fans' or 'breaking down the barriers' or whatever they choose to call it, but Peter actually put his body on the line.

It was inevitable, however, that the 'appearing at the back of the theatre' stunt would go wrong sooner or later. One night – I think we were in Pittsburgh – Peter and I headed out of the stage door and into the street, which was always a bit weird with all these buses and taxis everywhere and Peter in his white top clutching his radio mic. As usual the promoter's guy was waiting for us at the front of house but this particular theatre had two rows of glass doors, both of which could only be opened from the inside. Unfortunately, not being the sharpest knife in the drawer, this guy pushed the inner door open and forgot that it would shut automatically behind him. He let us in through the outer doors only to realise, too late, that the inner doors had closed behind him, leaving us trapped between the two banks of doors with no way back into the foyer. Peter and I watched in slow motion what was about to happen. 'Don't let it shut!' I screamed but I was too late. Luckily my cry wasn't picked up by Peter's radio mic.

Of course there was no one in the lobby as they were all inside enjoying the show and there was Peter, me and this bloke, locked out. We could faintly hear the band, so Peter was able to start singing when he heard his cue. Luckily there was a loo in the foyer and two guys walked out and saw us. We banged on the glass and mimed for all we were worth, 'LET US IN!' and of course they couldn't believe what they were seeing. 'What the fuck... Peter Gabriel's supposed to be on stage... what's he doing here?' They hesitated for a moment then ran forward to let us in. We didn't do the upstairs bit that night, just the walk down the aisle, and the audience – apart from the two blokes who'd been in the Gents – was none the wiser. The band knew something was up as they could hear him singing, but they were thinking, 'Where the hell is he?' We did that stunt every night on the whole tour, US and Europe, and it never went wrong again but I always included the double-door possibility in my preparations. To this day, my blood can still run cold when I think about that door closing in front of us.

This is not to say that other things didn't go wrong. By its very nature touring the world with a bunch of high-spirited musicians, an overworked road crew and thousands of pounds worth of delicate electronic equipment, all of which needs to be transported from city to city on a strict schedule, is no picnic. The margin of error is tiny, the chance of disaster enormous. Tour managers can prepare for the expected but the unexpected is all part of the game.

In Europe, we travelled in three Mercedes Benz 230 SE cars that became progressively muddier as the tour went on, largely because it was winter, cold, wet and occasionally snowbound. For part of the tour we were joined by some of the wives and girlfriends (WAGS), which occasionally led to tricky situations for the tour manager. I've heard tales of bands insisting that group members accompanied by their WAGS stay in separate hotels, a precautionary measure against reports going back to those at home about shenanigans on tour. No such complications ever disturbed the domestic harmony of my friends in Genesis. Being on the road can be extremely challenging for anyone not directly involved in the production. Inevitably, wives and girlfriends become camp followers with no function beyond soothing the troubled psyches of their musician rock star partners. They are expected to do what the road manager asks them and some don't take to this as readily as others. The road manager can find himself in the difficult position of receiving complaints and demands that are hard to deal with. From my point of view, the lower their profile the better. Margaret Banks was perfect. Teri Levin, Tony Levin's first wife, was ideal too. But our guitarist's wife Cindy did not enjoy or surrender to being a wife on the road, so she and Sid took one of the Mercedes and made their own way from Germany to France. As a result, they missed out on being hauled off at gunpoint by zealous Swiss police under the impression that our party comprised members of the Baader-Meinhof terrorist group.

We were in Munich. The next gig was in Besançon, where Peter performed his last ever show with Genesis. We had to drive through Switzerland into France to reach the town, a longish stretch of four or five hours. With Sid and Cindy well ahead of us, our other two cars were in convoy: Tony, Teri, Peter and me in one; Bayeté, Larry and Jerry in the other. To a casual observer we were a mixed crew, some might say a rum-looking bunch, all seven of us magnificent in our idiosyncratic prime – Bayeté, a black guy with a big afro, Jerry looking like a Mexican bandito with his droopy moustache and Tony Levin with his shaved head, an early example of a style that has now become ubiquitous.

We stopped in the small Swiss town of St Gallen for lunch. Afterwards Peter needed to call Gail Colson and made his way to a phone box near where I had parked our grubby Mercedes. As previously noted, Peter has never had the most robust of voices and in order for it to withstand the challenge of singing night after night on tour, his Harley Street doctor had advised he keep his throat warm at all times. Accordingly, he was wearing his Charterhouse scarf (blue with pink stripes) wrapped around his face, looking suspiciously as if he might be trying to conceal his identity.

Unfortunately this drew the attention of the good burghers of St Gallen who leapt on the idea that he could be a member of the notorious Baader-Meinhof gang.

This group of anti-capitalist terrorists had recently kidnapped Hanns Martin Schleyer, a German industrialist, and murdered him in cold blood before dumping his body on waste ground on the outskirts of Stuttgart. While the whole of Europe was on red alert it appeared that the people of St Gallen were convinced we were the terrorists. (We later found out that the police had received at least a dozen phone calls about us.)

Unaware of the drama that was about to unfold, I was sitting in the car playing a little game, one of those small wooden boxes with a glass lid where you roll balls around and try and get them into the holes. Next thing I knew, between me and the game appeared a gun. I looked up to discover that we were totally surrounded by armed police and soldiers. We were ordered out of our cars, firearms trained on us and arrested at gunpoint.

Everyone was extremely nervous, including the police, as we very slowly emerged from our two cars with our hands up. We were bundled into two police wagons, taken to the station and the interrogation began. 'Who are you? What are you doing? Where are you travelling from and to?' They searched my briefcase. This was before the days of the euro and, as was customary, the road manager's briefcase contained among other things a good deal of cash – about £5000 in half a dozen assorted European currencies. To them, this must have looked very suspicious. We tried to explain that we were musicians. 'Where are your instruments?' they asked, quite reasonably. We told them that the road crew had gone ahead and were already in Besançon setting up for tonight's concert.

In the event, we were not formally arrested, nor were we thrown into cells. The police soon realised we were English and American, not German. We sat in the reception of the police station, waiting patiently and politely while they brought our cars into the yard and thoroughly searched them. Because they thought we were armed terrorists, this was the focus of their search, so they overlooked a small quantity of dope that Bayeté had in his bag. Had they discovered it, this story would have had a very different outcome. By now, we had been the guests of the St Gallen police for a couple of hours. As part of their search, they again turned their attention to my briefcase, which turned out to be a good thing.

Ten days before, we had played a gig in Bern, the capital of Switzerland. Andy the promoter, being true to his national stereotype, was incredibly efficient and meticulous with his paperwork. When we arrived at the venue in Bern he had handed me a dossier with a whole load of documents pertaining to the show. I never looked at them, just shoved them into the back of my briefcase. If I had one ounce of Andy's efficiency, I would have thrown that folder out as soon as we moved on after the Bern gig. But I didn't and it turned out to be our salvation. Unbeknownst to me, the folder contained a copy of a Bern police document giving the necessary permission for the concert to go ahead and, to cap it all, it had all the band members' names on it. This was our get-out-of-jail card. So, in spite of having no instruments and looking like the rum bunch we were, this official document proved our identity. They couldn't hold us any longer.

Next, we needed to get in touch with the crew in Besançon. The police, who had lightened up considerably after scanning the document from Bern, allowed us to make a phone call to the crew and explain what had happened. If we left right away, we could make it to the gig in France in time for the show. Sid, having driven ahead with Cindy, would have to do the sound check on behalf of the whole band as the audience would already be in the hall by the time we got there.

There was only one thing left to do before we bid adieu to our friends from the St Gallen *gendarmerie*. Peter started his shows on this tour with an a cappella rendition of a novelty song called 'Excuse Me'. So it was, that right there in the police reception area, we gave them a rousing rendition of that cheery song. Then we said our goodbyes, handshakes all round, leapt into our cars and sped off towards France. We made it just in time for the band to throw on their costumes and leap on stage. The audience were none the wiser and the show went down a storm.

It would be misleading to portray that particular incident, dramatic as it was, as an own goal occasioned by a harassed tour manager's carelessness, but the same cannot be said of what occurred in Rotterdam a few nights later.

It will probably come as no surprise to you that certain individuals within the rock fraternity have been known to benefit or suffer – depending on your point of view – from the use of illegal drugs. Certain substances might inspire creativity, often giving rise to surreal imagery, while others might pacify a troubled mind, acting as an aid to slumber or prolonging wakefulness. It is this latter effect that is much appreciated by members of the crew when they are called upon to keep going well beyond what might be considered normal working hours.

In any event, it was considered part of the road manager's job to provide such drugs as might be regarded beneficial for the crew and any band members who wanted them. In fact, very few of the musicians were interested, but the poor old crew definitely needed assistance. They had to load in, do the gig, load out and get on the bus to the next show, snatching what sleep they could while driving all night, and do it all over again the next day, quite often eight or ten days in a row. The more we kept going the better since days off were incredibly expensive. As if paying out with nothing coming in was bad enough, some form of sickness would tend to break out if the routine was interrupted. I was not alone in my trade in believing that a day off was a disaster waiting to happen. It did happen, though not in the manner I anticipated.

We stayed for two nights in Rotterdam, the Dutch port that also happens to be the centre of Europe's drug trade and enjoyed a free day before the night of the show. The promoter was doing a concert with the US band Chicago on our night off, so with the complimentary tickets that he kindly provided most of us went to watch the Windy City's jazz rock pioneers. It was a welcome break for the crew but it was communicated to me that a booster shot might help shore up their exertions over the next few days, and they weren't talking about Vitamin B-12.

So it was that through a connection in Rotterdam, a dealer who in this instance was, perhaps atypically, a charming young woman, came to my hotel room after the second of our two shows and after a bit of bargaining agreed to deliver about 27 grams – a considerable amount of what was euphemistically known in the business as 'Peruvian marching powder'. Once the deal was done, I set about separating the white powder into individual 'wraps' (packets) which I placed in an envelope that I secreted in the back flap of my briefcase. Having succumbed to the temptation of sampling the goods, I went to bed very late and had a short and restless night.

The next morning we checked out of the hotel, me with my briefcase on the counter, sorting out the bills for the rooms, scrutinising each one to see that no one had been overcharged or, indeed, had helped themselves to the towelling bathrobes – all part of the usual routine for a harassed manager on too little sleep. It probably didn't help my concentration when some of the guys from Chicago arrived to check out themselves, a distraction that would cause no little anxiety down the line. Final tasks accomplished, we headed for Brussels, the next gig on the itinerary, with Peter and Gail in my car and the rest in the other two vehicles. Because the crew had already left, I would distribute the boosters to them later at that night's show.

It was when we were checking into the Brussels hotel that I realised how catastrophically careless I had been. To my horror I had left my briefcase containing the drugs at the checkout counter in the lobby of the Rotterdam Hilton. I had to hide my mounting panic from Peter and Gail who no doubt believed the contents of the case to be largely innocuous.

I went up to my hotel room and called the Hilton in Rotterdam where it was confirmed that the briefcase had been found and safely set aside in the porter's lodge. Next, I called the Dutch promoter who arranged for a taxi driver to collect it and drive to Brussels, hopefully to deliver it into my hands. Unlike my parents, I don't adhere to traditional religious beliefs but once I was in my room I earnestly uttered a silent prayer. If the briefcase were searched by customs officers at the border between the Netherlands and Belgium, I would almost certainly be charged with drug trafficking; the quantity inside that case was well above the maximum that is deemed suitable for personal use. Like Peter's, my heart was going boom, boom, boom!

Luck was on my side. The taxi driver was stopped at the border but when the customs officer asked about the contents of the briefcase, he simply and truthfully said he had no idea what was inside and was merely delivering it to someone in Brussels. Looking back, I am absolutely astounded that it wasn't searched. To have engaged a taxi to deliver a case from Rotterdam to Brussels, at no little expense, was surely deeply suspicious. It could have contained anything – diamonds, explosives, wads of cash (there was quite a lot of that as it happened), not to mention illegal drugs.

Phew! I could have been locked up for years. My guardian angel was definitely looking out for me that day but I was beginning to wonder how long I could keep up this lifestyle. Maybe a change was coming…

Chapter 15

I DIDN'T CHOOSE
BRAND X

So, every morning on that tour
I would wake up to find my naked roommate
leaping around the room …

After the farce of Peter being locked out of his own concert and us all being mistaken for homicidal terrorists, not to mention the temporary but excruciating separation from my briefcase with its compromising contents, it was something of a relief to get back to my life in Trellick Tower, contemplating West London far below without having to worry about the next night's concert, and the next, and the next.

I had fallen into the role of tour manager almost by accident, a continuation of my friendship with my school friends and had become pretty adept at it over the years. Nevertheless, the issue of whether or not I wanted to continue in this role with Peter was troubling me and in imitation of my dear friend, I was vacillating. To be a friend or an employee, that was the question. Forsooth, I must make up my mind. But I didn't, at least not for the time being.

I was to be given a taste of what it was like working outside of the Genesis circle when Tony Smith asked me to take Brand X on a short tour of America. Brand X was Phil Collins's jazz rock pursuit on the side; as a full-time staff member of Hit & Run, Tony Smith and Gail Colson's management company, I could hardly refuse.

Peter was down in Bath writing material for 'Melt'; he didn't need me so I was fully up for Brand X's first foray to the States.

Phil is genetically incapable of idleness. He never took a day off. Even when we were on the road with Genesis for 12 days straight, the following day when everyone else would be resting, he'd tell me he needed his drum kit because he was doing a session somewhere. Brand X had come in to being after Phil met a musician called Robin Lumley, a jazz keyboard player and record producer, who also happened to be a cousin of *Ab Fab's* Joanna Lumley. Phil and Robin had formed a powerful jazz rock outfit that was modelled on John McLaughlin's Mahavishnu Orchestra or Chick Corea's Return to Forever. It was a similar kind of vibe: fast and furious, very jazzy, very technical, an amazing band as it happens though, as it turned out, they were doomed because of Phil's conflicting loyalties. As well as Robin and Phil, there was Percy Jones, a brilliant bass player, John Goodsall, a fine guitarist, and a Scottish percussionist called Morris Pert who was one of those supremely musical percussionists whose palette extended to marimbas, vibes and keyboards.

They were indeed an impressive outfit; they had an album out on Charisma in May 1977 called *Moroccan Roll*, which actually got into the Top 40 – quite an achievement for complex and somewhat cerebral music (though I guess Phil's involvement gave it a head start). The US tour that followed was in June and July of the same year.

In many ways this was a fill-in position for me, something to do before Peter was ready to tour again. Contrary to my previous experiences on the road, this wasn't a happy tour for me. First, disastrously, there was no Phil. He was too busy with other things and couldn't come, so it was Brand X without Phil, the main reason why anyone in the world was interested in the group. Consequently we had to employ a stand-in drummer and to avoid the exchange rule imposed by the Musicians' Union, instead of taking a musician from the UK, we picked one up in America, a guy called Kenwood (Woody) Dennard, a talented and congenial black jazz drummer from New Jersey.

The second reason for my distress was that I did not get on with Robin Lumley. In a nutshell, he was really pissed off that he had to do this tour without Phil and in many ways I can't blame him. He saw Brand X as his ticket to fame and fortune but this was not going to happen without the main attraction. Of course, the first thing that everybody asked when they got to a gig was, 'Where's Phil?' Woody had a t-shirt made up after the first show with 'Where's Phil?' printed on the front. It was a good joke but it didn't help my relationship with teeth-gnashing Robin.

Things got off to a bad start even before the first gig. The band members, mostly strangers to New York, wanted to stay at the Chelsea Hotel, at that time a horrible dump, very famous and full of legend and folklore but without any charm as far as I was concerned. I said, 'All right, it's not what I would recommend but we'll do it if you insist.' Of course it was summer, boiling hot with no air conditioning. We spent one night there and the next morning they were all begging me to take them somewhere where there weren't people screaming in the corridors all night long and so I booked us into to the good old Gorham on 55th Street, which is where I had wanted to stay in the first place. As ever, it was bliss: air-conditioned, Carnegie Deli round the corner, close to Hit & Run's New York office.

The office was really a support structure for Genesis who by now were becoming massive. It was run by a good friend of mine, Dick Fraser, who was King Crimson's first roadie, no doubt wrestling with the same enormous Mellotron that had made my life a misery when Genesis first acquired one. Dick sent me to see Mike Farrell at the William Morris Agency who gave me the Brand X itinerary – three weeks worth of dates in clubs that held about 200 people, with tables and chairs and a tiny stage often too small to accommodate Morris Pert's extensive percussion set-up. These clubs had their own PA systems and my job as sound mixer was made easy; there were no vocals compared to Genesis or Peter. These clubs were markedly different to the venues we were used to. The band typically played two 45-minute sets and in between, out would come pitchers of beer and towering burgers with buckets of French fries which the crowd would devour. I drove a minibus for the band and a truck driven by a crew of two transported the equipment. The tour comprised East Coast and Midwest dates only. We played in New York, Boston, Philly, Washington DC, the usual cities, and got as far as a Chicago suburb called Schaumberg, where the gig was in a club called Beginnings, owned by Chicago's drummer, Danny Seraphino.

This tour was running on the proverbial shoestring, so we shared rooms. As the others were all paired up I shared with Woody, the drummer. One of the great things about going to New York in those days was being able to buy electronic devices from Japan that weren't yet available in England. It seems ridiculous now, in the days of smart phones, but I was really excited when I got my hands on a little Casio calculator and alarm clock. One of the tricks it could do was to tell you what day of the week you were born on if you keyed in your birthday and year. Amazing... well, it was then. I used it as an alarm clock and tolerated the only sound it made, a very annoying electronic beeping noise that would go off first thing in the morning.

Now it might come as a surprise to learn that my new friend Woody was profoundly deaf. Even though he was a young guy and a drummer, he wore two large hearing aids. Of course, he didn't sleep with them on, but for some reason he could hear the electronic beeping of my prized new toy very clearly. He would wake up in a frenzy trying to locate it. If he'd done so no doubt he would have smashed it to pieces. So every morning on that tour I would wake up to find my naked roommate leaping around the room trying to find the instrument that was torturing him. Fortunately he never found it.

Woody and I got on very well but Robin Lumley seemed determined to make my life a misery. He was a producer and writer and had used the band members to record jingles, so they were all very dependent on him. This meant that none of them would stand up to him, though at one point during the tour both Percy and Morris apologised to me for the way Robin was behaving.

Looking back at the situation from Robin's point of view, I can understand his frustration; Brand X could have been really big, as big as Mahavishnu, but not without Phil's full commitment. I had become the repository for this irritation. Genesis at that point were getting bigger and bigger and no way was Phil going to prioritise Brand X. For him it was just a bit of fun. Nevertheless, the album recorded by these great musicians stands as a very decent piece of work and the tour was successful in its limited way. Mixing the sound every night, I could hear with my own ears how good they were.

The biggest show we did on the Brand X tour was supporting Supertramp in a venue that held up to 10,000 people in Norfolk, Virginia. The best thing about it was getting there via the Chesapeake Bay Bridge-Tunnel. This mighty piece of engineering starts off as a bridge and suddenly, part way across, a hole opens up and you drive down under the seabed to clear a lane for the shipping because it's the home of the US Navy. There are huge ships coming in and out the whole time. Then you emerge again for a while above the water to find another tunnel for the second shipping lane before you come off the bridge and into Norfolk. It's 12 miles long, built to replace the ferries that used to take the traffic before the Second World War.

I say that this was the best thing about the gig because the show itself was probably the low point of the whole tour (though after my experiences with Peter and Genesis it was interesting to see it all from the perspective of being a humble support act). Being a support act in America is like being thrown a crumb from the great table. The members of Supertramp won't have known about the friction between the camps but their crew saw us simply as a nuisance. Just by being there we caused them extra work they didn't want to have to do in order to accommodate us and they didn't go out their way to be helpful. They refused to move any of their stage gear so we had to fit onto whatever space they left for us, which was minimal. We didn't get a chance to do a sound check because the main band took up all the time available, so when they'd finished, we wheeled our stuff on stage and set it up as best we could while the audience began to trickle in. Also, though I may be being a little paranoid here, it isn't unknown for the sound engineer for the top band to switch on only a part of the sound system. What it boils down to is that you don't look good, you don't sound good and no one's really listening anyway.

So Norfolk was a bum gig and I haven't even mentioned that when we started our set there was a terrible hum on the PA and my hands were tied. I couldn't exactly turn round to the sound engineer and ask, 'Excuse me old chap, can you do something about that hum please?' He'd have laughed in my face. Of course the hum had mysteriously disappeared by the time Supertramp came on. I'll never know whether it was deliberate sabotage or an accidental cock-up but it certainly didn't enhance my reputation with Robin Lumley. It simply gave him another stick to beat me with.

Mind you it does sometimes happen that the support band can blow the headliners off stage. It happened with Ike & Tina Turner when they came on before the Stones. They didn't blow the Stones off exactly but they were so amazing with the Ikettes that the audience would never forget them. Little Feat did the same thing to the Doobie Brothers at the Rainbow in London in 1974. As for Led Zeppelin on their first tour of America, after a handful of support gigs no one in the world wanted to follow them. Everyone was terrified not only of the band but the growing ugly reputation of their road crew.

But I digress. When I got back to the London office after the tour, a surprisingly positive outcome awaited me. I was told by the accountant at Hit & Run, a guy called Brian Murray-Smith, that the tour only lost 500 dollars. For a first American tour by any kind of band that was pretty impressive, and for a jazz-rock group it was remarkable. By then I had learned how to keep a tight rein on expenses. I had friends in New York who gave me good advice and I was hip to ways to save money, tricks like renting trucks from New Jersey because of the different tax structure that wasn't available in the state of New York. A few weeks after the tour, Robin Lumley apologised to me for the way he had behaved. He came into the office, and said, 'I behaved badly. I'm really sorry.

It wasn't your fault. You did really well.' It was nice to hear that from him.

There was one other thing that stood out on that trip, and it had nothing to do with Brand X, Woody or Robin. I saw the first *Star Wars* movie for the first time, long before it reached the UK. Walter from the Hit & Run office told us about it and so off I went with Morris and Percy. When we pitched up outside the cinema on 44th Street you could tell that there was a definite buzz in the air, that the movie was something special. We bought our tickets and, still somewhat innocent, I went into the gents where, believe it or not, there was a guy selling single joints for a dollar. I bought one, sat down in the cinema and contentedly smoked it. No one cared about that sort of thing in those days, in fact they sold them outside gigs. This meant that music places often smelled like a gigantic marijuana smoke-in, not unlike The Paradiso in Amsterdam.

So there I was happily stoned with this incredible film unfolding in front of me and at that moment when the Millennium Falcon does the jump to light speed, well, no one had ever seen anything like it before! The whole place went bananas; there was a standing ovation. I returned to England and banged on about *Star Wars* for months. When the film subsequently came out in a blaze of publicity, it was a bit of a let down when I finally went to see it with my friends. I'd had the advantage of knowing nothing about it first time round and this was too overwhelming an experience to repeat.

Back at Trellick, I was unhappily mulling over my first non-Genesis touring experience. I couldn't help but conclude that I really only liked doing this job if I was working for Genesis or a Genesis offshoot. With Brand X, once Phil wasn't there, it wasn't even an offshoot but a completely separate tree. Then came Peter Gabriel's next tour with all the stresses and strains described in the previous chapter.

After that, sucker for punishment that I was, I did the same job for Peter Hammill, late of Van Der Graaf Generator, which is one removed from a Genesis offshoot, but still a Charisma act and still managed by Gail at Hit & Run. Once again it was a US tour that visited many of the same venues as the Brand X outing, at least on the East Coast and in the Midwest. In fact, it was a breeze as far as the personnel were concerned – just Peter H with his guitar and a portable electric piano, and a violinist called Graham Smith who had made a name for himself with String Driven Thing. So we were four, the musicians, me and an American roadie called Dale Newman who had previously made himself indispensable as guitar technician to Genesis. On this tour, Dale looked after the gear while I once again mixed the sound. We all travelled in a van that became our window on to the magnificence of the ever-changing great American landscape.

By this time Peter Hammill had released several solo albums, all of them recorded in his home studio near Bradford on Avon. This tour was designed to promote one called *PH7*, which was actually his eighth. Perverse character that he is, PH7 refers to the balance of alkaline and acidity in our bodies – or so I was led to believe. The tour opened on the East Coast and finished in San Francisco, a coast-to-coast trip undertaken perhaps optimistically in late winter, February 1979.

I say optimistically because the gig in Boston was followed by another impressive Nor'easter snowstorm and in the morning there was some doubt as to whether we'd make the gig in Philadelphia. But I knew from past experience that once you get on to the highways in America it's usually plain sailing – remember the trip with Jill Gabriel and the girls a while back – and we got to Philly in good shape. We arrived triumphant only to discover that the gig had been cancelled. 'But we've just driven all the way from Boston,' I told the promoter. 'What's the bloody problem mate?' The thing was you couldn't get out of your own street because it hadn't been ploughed but if you could get on to the freeway you could go anywhere you wanted.

Hitches like that aside, it was a fun tour. We drove right the way across America. The further west we got the greater the distances and the fewer the gigs. We had a gig in Phoenix and by the time we got there the sun was out and we were swimming in the hotel pool. We then proceeded to drive across Arizona, taking in the Meteor Crater and the Petrified Forest, finally arriving in Los Angeles.

At a friend's wedding
with Maggie – thank you to
Tony Sleep for the photo.

Maggie admiring a hibiscus flower in Seville, 1987.

Richard Macphail – Friend and Road Manager

My moment of fame from the Genesis documentary –
thanks to Chris Bridges for the capture.

With Phil Collins and Steve Hackett at
the premier of the BBC Genesis documentary.
Thank you to Jo Hackett for the photo.

On holiday with Peter
and Jill Gabriel in Corfu, 1979.

Jerry Marotta in the
Hotel Negresco, Nice.
On tour with Peter Gabriel.

On tour in Italy with Peter Hammill, me pretending to play the guitar.

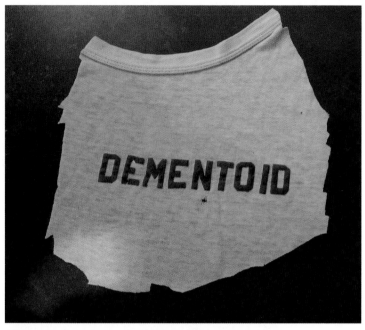

All that remains of the t-shirt that Peter Hammill had made for me during the Peter Tosh tour of Italy in 1978.

1977 Canal du Midi holiday with
From left: RPM, Teri Levin, Janessa and Tony Levin.

The LA gigs were followed by the last show in San Francisco where I had the good fortune to meeting a young woman with whom I felt a connection. Naomi was a graphic artist living on a houseboat in Sausalito. I invited her back to our hotel and we spent a delightful night together. Like a lot of people in California, she had come from the East Coast. She had attended art school in the San Francisco area and soon after been offered a good job so she had stayed on to make her life out there. In my time as a roadie I had very few encounters like that so it was all the more precious. It made the parting the next day sharper as Dale and I had to climb aboard our van to start the long drive back to New York. Peter and Graham flew straight back to London from SF.

We took it in turns to drive and sleep, one of us kipping in the back with the gear, the other taking the wheel. Having invested in a Citizens Band (CB) radio we got a great kick out of feeling connected to the truckers on the freeway warning each other about highway patrols or 'smoky' as they called them. Wyoming brought us another mammoth American snowfall, forcing us to pull off in a place called Laramie where we found a motel, slept for six hours and somehow managed to avoid the local cowboys who might not have taken kindly to long hairs like us. We left San Francisco on a Saturday morning and reached New York the following Tuesday night, pretty good going, though I was stopped for speeding along the way, something that has been a bit of a theme in my life.

I never used to speak into our CB radio because I figured that my English public school accent might cause some truckers to die laughing and drive off the road. What I learned from listening to them was that you had to watch the mile markers that appear along the side of the freeway. They would say something like, 'There's smoky on the side in a plain wrapper taking pictures at 147,' meaning there was a highway patrol in an unmarked car using his radar at mile marker 147. That would tell me where to slow down, or that was the theory. It didn't always work. The speed limit was 55 mph in America in those days so the temptation to go a bit faster, especially when you had a couple of thousand miles ahead of you, was difficult to resist. When I got pulled over and was sitting in the police car, the moment I opened my mouth they were all over me. 'Where are you from buddy boy? Say something. Heh-heh-heh. I gotta take you back to see the judge 'cos he's gonna love the way you talk.' On top of that the highway patrolman looking at my licence was listening to CB radio and I heard a truck driver saying, 'Oh, there's that van that overtook us a mile back. I'm not surprised he's been pulled over.' It's a funny world. I don't think I ever paid a fine. It was just the inconvenience of being stopped.

Despite such interruptions, it took us just four days to get the van and the equipment back to New York. While I was working on this book in June 2017, I ran into Dale Newman at Anthony Phillips's house. We reminisced about the Peter Hammill tour and he said that it was the most pleasant one he's ever done.

After the tour was over I flew home for another adventure with Peter Hammill. This one was in Italy where, for reasons that don't merit close scrutiny, he was booked to appear as support act to Peter Tosh, once a third of The Wailers with Bob Marley and Bunny Livingstone, now forging his own way in the world with a bit of help from Mick Jagger, who had signed him to Rolling Stones Records and duetted with him on his only hit, '(You Gotta Walk) Don't Look Back', in 1978.

The ill-matched pairing of Tosh and Hammill came about because Peter H was friendly with an agent called Gordian Troeller who had fixed up the tour for Peter Tosh. He was a big star at the time thanks to his hit with Jagger, and was coming from Jamaica to play Italian football stadia over the summer of 1979 with Sly Dunbar and Robbie Shakespeare on bass and drums, the best reggae rhythm section in the business. Gordian happened to mention to Peter H that there was no support act and perhaps not realising what he was in for, he said he would do it. Unfortunately this was only a week before the tour started and although Peter had quite a decent following in Italy, his name wasn't on any of the posters. Consequently none of his own fans knew he was doing these gigs and of course, none of them showed up. Italian reggae fans did though, in their thousands.

So off we went again, just Peter and me and a bit of gear. The Tosh crew were all Brits picked up in London, so they kindly offered to take Peter's keyboard and guitar with them in one of their trucks. Peter and I were content to take the crew's coach, Dover to Calais, through France and then, once again, over the Alps down into Italy.

Well, for Peter Hammill it was just awful. The audiences loathed him. Peter is very much an acquired taste; his angst-ridden songs appeal to a very specific kind of fan – not really the kind of act to put before a crowd of Italian reggae lovers who are out for a good time dancing to the bass-heavy beat. All sorts of stuff would rain down on the stage when he was on. To this day – and I don't say this lightly – I've never seen courage like it. Knowing precisely what was going to happen, he went on fearlessly, night after night and faced down those reggae crowds.

Tosh's tour manager was sympathetic to Peter's plight but a bit inexperienced in the ways of the road and I found myself having to pull rank in Brescia, where the promoter, to save money, had failed to provide a roof over the stage. Said promoter, a guy called Willie Mamoni, was reputed to have pulled a gun on Uriah Heep during a dispute about money some years earlier. He was a bit of a sinister character but I liked him even though it was clear that if you got on the wrong side of him, things could quickly take a dark turn. So there we were, about to unload half a million pounds worth of delicate equipment with cloud covered mountains all around us and thunder rumbling ominously in the distance. 'Oh, it never rains in August in Italy,' says Willie but I didn't believe him. 'This is ridiculous,' I respond. 'Who's gonna pay for all this gear if it does?' I knew from my tours with Genesis that when it rains in Italy in the summer it pelts down for at least 20 minutes and woe betide any amp that gets drenched as a result.

During this difference of opinion, Tosh's tour manager was looking at me as if I was risking my life, but Willy eventually saw the sense of it, probably because any equipment damage would be down to him. He very sensibly put the show back to the end of the tour, adding a roof over the stage. Peter Tosh did have a manager (it was rumoured) but it turned out that as soon as he'd arrived in Europe he had flown straight to Munich to buy spare parts for his BMW back in Jamaica. I only got to meet him on the last day of the tour in Naples. While in the neighbourhood, Peter H and I went up Vesuvius, which was becoming a habit of mine by now. At the end of the tour Peter nicknamed me Dementoid and gave me a t-shirt with that emblazoned on the front. I treasured it for years and my wife Maggie used to sleep in it. It still exists in a faded parchment-like state.

The only other tour I did during this period was a short trip to France with a few dates in Germany with the drummer Bill Bruford. As I've said, Bill started out in Yes and then went behind the kit in Genesis when Phil became the front man after Peter Gabriel left; he's also part of the King Crimson family. Bill is an intellectual guy who takes life very seriously and I liked him a lot. It goes without saying that he became close friends with Tony Banks who shares the same attributes.

Bill put together a stunning jazz rock band which featured among others, Dave Stewart from Hatfield & the North on keyboards and an unbelievable American bass player called Jeff Berlins, one of the most remarkable musicians I've ever come across. He would dazzle us all in the dressing room by effortlessly running up and down the scales of any suggested key on his fretless bass. Jeff was astonishing. I only did one tour with them but it was a lot of fun.

It was now time for me to return to my flat in the sky and once again ponder my future while looking out over the cars and buses that clogged up the streets of Notting Hill and the boats that floated on the waterways at Paddington Basin and the Grand Union Canal. I still hadn't resolved my dilemma with the other Peter, he of the angelic surname. Would I continue to work for him or continue as his friend, probably the longest standing friendship he had? It was really a no brainer.

Chapter 16

BIRDS ON THE WIRE

---

*'It's Van Morrison for you,' she said,
her eyes like saucers. 'I'm coming up to London,'
he informed me. 'Meet me at the West London air
terminal, eight o'clock tonight.' It was the kind of
summons you might expect from MI5.*

I finally told Peter Gabriel that I no longer wanted to work for him; the next time he went out on the road he would have to find a new tour manager. I don't think his heart was broken by the news. He understood where I was coming from and therefore didn't beg me to stay. I'm sure he wouldn't have denied that he was difficult to work for and that I needed to draw a line in the sand between our friendship and my experience as a tour manager. The wisdom of my decision is reflected in the fact that Peter and I are still the best of friends and bearing in mind how far back we go, back to those less than wonderful days at Charterhouse, this is something that I hold as precious.

Peter or no Peter, I was still on the staff of Hit & Run and occasionally found myself being farmed out as a hired hand to anyone who needed me. Sometimes this was fun, sometimes it wasn't. Sometimes it was just plain weird or at least slightly bewildering. Into this latter category must fall my brief tenure as personal assistant to none other than Van 'The Man' Morrison, of taciturn Irish disposition, *Astral Weeks* and 'Brown Eyed Girl'.

Tony Smith had business dealings with Harvey Goldsmith who had become the UK's foremost concert promoter after Tony Smith opted out of promoting in favour of Genesis, coupled with the retirement of his father John. Harvey, in addition to being the UK's top concert promoter liked to dabble in artist management. Intrepid optimist that he was, in 1977 he became the manager of Van Morrison (in spite of Van's reputation for also being difficult to work with). He rang me to say he was looking for a 'perse' for Van and would I be interested. Well, of course I was, if for no other reason than I've always loved Them's 'Baby, Please Don't Go'. His bluesy voice with its Irish edge, his bracingly authentic lyrics and the raw sound of the band added up to something genuinely new and different. A little footnote: the cracking guitar intro to 'Baby, Please Don't Go' turned out, I discovered much later, to have been the work of Jimmy Page and not whoever played guitar in Them.

I rocked up at Harvey's offices and his PA gave me a book, *Van Morrison: Into the Music* by Canadian writer Ritchie Yorke, published in 1975 by – believe it or not – Charisma Books, one of Strat's many offshoots. This seemed like a good omen. Harvey was out so I sat in his reception and read it, learning much more about Van's background than I already knew. When Harvey came back he told me that Van had just finished making his *Period Of Transition* album, was living somewhere out in the Thames Valley with an American wife and needed someone to look after him. Harvey gave me his number and I called him up. We seemed to establish what I would describe as a cool relationship – cool as in slightly frosty as opposed to stylish. Van was what you might call laconic, never one to waste words, and the first thing he told me was that he didn't like driving in London. A couple of days later, the phone rang at Trellick Tower and my friend Cass answered the call. 'Is Richard there?' inquired a man with the thickest Belfast accent she'd ever heard. 'It's Van Morrison.' Well, Cass nearly fell off her chair. She handed me the phone with a look of disbelief. 'It's Van Morrison for you,' she said, her eyes like saucers. 'I'm coming up to London,' he informed me. 'Meet me at the West London air terminal, eight o'clock tonight.' Then he put the phone down. It was the kind of summons you might expect from MI5.

Back then, on Cromwell Road where there is now a Sainsbury's supermarket, there was an air terminal where you could check in for certain airlines. After leaving your bags there you could get on a coach to Heathrow, go straight through customs and on to the plane. Also, it just happened to be a convenient place to leave a car, parking in London having yet to develop into the time-consuming, expensive and potentially disastrous growth industry it is today.

So I drove down to the air terminal from Trellick and Van pulled up; I parked up and settled into the driver's seat of his car. 'We're going to Marble Arch,' he announced, so I headed up Park Lane and he directed me to a mews behind the Cumberland Hotel. 'Park here,' he said and we headed upstairs into a mews flat where two guys were waiting for us. The first was Chris Wood from Traffic and the second was Mac Rebennack, better known as Dr John. We were introduced, pleasantries were exchanged and the four of us returned to the car. 'We're going to Ronnie Scotts,' Van informed me, so off we drove towards Soho. We were there to experience the music of Rahsaan Roland Kirk, the blind saxophonist who played at least two saxes at once, sometimes three, all suspended from harnesses around his neck. The four of us sat at a table, listened to his set, had something to eat, drank a few bevies, then listened to the second set. Kirk was utterly amazing and my three new best friends were bowled over by his playing. There was no backstage meet and greet or anything like that. At the end we just came out, got back into the car and I drove them back to the flat at Marble Arch where we bade each other goodnight. I then took Van back to the West London air terminal where I waved him off and collected my car.

That was all I ever did for him. I worked for him for less than a month. You could probably count the number of words he said to me on the fingers of two hands. After another week he decided to move back to America and I had to arrange to have his stuff shipped. I got a removals firm to pack up all his belongings into a shipping container and went down to where he lived to pick him up on the day of the flight. I remember he had a lot of luggage, a hell of a lot, £250 worth of excess baggage as I recall. Fortunately I had a Hit & Run American Express card so I simply charged it to that. Then off he went on his Pan Am flight to Los Angeles and that was that.

Van Morrison's management deal with Harvey didn't last much longer than I did. Van actually asked Harvey to quit promoting concerts and move to LA but Harvey declined. 'When I can earn as much money out of you as I can at promoting, then I'll pack it up,' he told him, or so I read somewhere.

Years later, I was at the Ross-on-Wye festival where my wife Maggie was doing a recital in a church and in among the wide range of music on offer, was Van Morrison in a marquee for which the promoters gave us free tickets. He came on wearing his trademark fedora, played a great set, never said a word to the audience, just stood there and delivered. We were sitting slightly to the right of centre and I could see that there was a huge clock at the side of the stage, its digital display counting down to zero. It seems that he was contracted to play for 75 minutes and when the clock got to zero that was that, off he went without a second glance. He is an outstanding musician but his reputation as a tetchy fellow is certainly well earned, at least as far as my experience goes.

The same cannot be said of my final 'perse' client, the late Leonard Cohen, who turned out to be one of the most gracious superstars it has ever been my pleasure to encounter. I was contracted to manage his European tour, which ran from late 1979 into the early months of 1980, another assignment that came courtesy of Hit & Run.

Cohen's manager at the time was Marty Machat, a New York lawyer who represented Charisma in America and therefore was on good terms with Strat and Gail Colson. Another character straight out of Hollywood central casting, he was a classic music business attorney, sharp as a carving knife, wisecracking away but never taking his eye off the pots of gold that bounced around the industry. Whenever and wherever there was a fight going on between musicians and record companies over royalties, Marty would be in the thick of it, picking up a hefty fee from the generous scraps that landed on the floor.

For Leonard's European tour Marty, as his manager, had procured the services of a German promoter to set up all the dates. With Genesis and Peter we had always dealt with different promoters in each country, so this was a new and more streamlined way of doing things. The German tour manager, hired by our promoter, somehow wasn't to Leonard's liking and he had asked Marty to find someone else. Marty called Gail, Gail called me, and the next day I was on a plane to Gothenburg to pick up the tour. 'Hello Leonard, I'm Richard,' and happily we clicked from the word go. He was a lovely guy, though at this stage in his life he was drinking a considerable amount of Remy Martin brandy every day. Even with that inside him he was unfailingly charming, funny and courteous. He had an unstoppable creative flow.

Leonard's most recent album, accurately but rather prosaically entitled *Recent Songs*, had been recorded with a jazz-rock-R&B group called Passenger from Austin, Texas. The band was formed by Texan bassist Roscoe Beck, who remained Leonard's musical director up to the time of his death. Cohen's band included Mitch Watkins on guitar, Paul Ostermayer on saxophone, Steve Meador on drums, Bill Ginn on keyboards, violinist Raffi Hakopian, and oud and mandolin player John Bilezikjian, along with vocalists Jennifer Warnes and Sharon Robinson, the last of whom would also become a regular co-writer with Leonard. Needless to say, it was an absolutely top-notch band and somewhat unusual as well.

John Bilezikjian was an Armenian Californian, a staggering musician, well-covered and jolly, who played his oud on the bus between gigs, plucking it with a condor quill rather than a plectrum. He existed in a world far removed from contemporary pop. 'I didn't even know who The Beatles were until I met my wife,' he told one Cohen biographer. Raffi was Russian. He spoke no English so music was the only language in which he communicated with the rest of the band. Jennifer Warnes had just released her album, *Shot Through the Heart*, which had shot into the US top 20. It is a testament to her friendship with Lenny and her high regard for his art that she chose to go on this European tour with him rather than promoting her own album. Needless to say, her record company people were tearing their hair out. Jennifer and Sharon, with their astounding voices, created their own version of the trademark Leonard back-up vocal style – smooth, sexy and somewhat ironic. One of the greatest joys of this tour were the times when we all sang together on the long bus rides. A particular song Jennifer taught us was the classic American hymn to the poor, 'Hard Times' by Steven Foster, which has become a strong tradition to sing around our Thanksgiving table at home.

After Gothenburg the tour visited France, Belgium, Germany, Switzerland and England. Leonard and his band performed 53 concerts in 44 cities in less than 70 days with a comprehensive set-list of 45 songs to draw from. The show included an interval and at the beginning of the second half he would appear on stage with just a guitar and totally mesmerise his audience, weaving a spell as he played older songs from his catalogue. Then, bit by bit, the band would come back on stage and join in with the newer material.

One thing that struck me on this tour more than any other that I ever managed was the age range of his audience – well-dressed middle-aged couples mingling with students in jeans and t-shirts. I'm probably not the first observer to note how rock'n'roll has destroyed the generation gap that used to exist between parents and their children. Performers like Leonard Cohen really do appeal to all ages. On that theme, I'll always remember when Genesis did a UK tour of small theatres and played at the Southampton Gaumont. A friend of mine noticed a car pull up outside and an old grey-haired guy get out. The young driver shouted, 'I'll come back and pick you up later, Dad.'

But back to Leonard and what for me was a dream tour. I didn't have to mix the sound. I didn't even have to do the accounts, which used to be a pain in the neck in Europe in those days because of all the different currencies we had to juggle. Amazingly, the road manager that Leonard didn't like stayed on in the background and was happy to deal with the money, which he executed with brilliant Germanic efficiency.

So this was the last tour I ever managed, and one of the happiest as well.

MY BOOK OF GENESIS

Chapter 17

A MARRIAGE
OF CONVENIENCE

*The moment came when, on returning from a trip
to the US, an immigration official disappeared into the
glass box with Maggie's passport for a long time.
When he finally handed it back, it came with the strong
but surprising advice that if she wanted to stay any
longer, she should marry a Brit.*

After the Leonard Cohen tour that ended on such a high, I opted
out of the tour managing game altogether. In fact before that tour
started I had optimistically decided to give my singing career
one more crack of the whip. This had always been in the back
of my mind but somehow Genesis and its various offshoots had
thoroughly occupied me.

Following in the great tradition of the era, I scanned the *Melody
Maker* looking for a group that needed a singer and, sure enough,
discovered one in Hemel Hempstead called MC². The leader of the
band was a guitarist called Murray Munro and his daughter Sarah,
now a singer of some repute herself, says that her dad remembers
me arriving for the audition. To quote Murray:

We put an advert in the Melody Maker *for a singer and held
auditions at our drummer Mike Harris's parents' house. Richard
turned up on a motorbike in a black leather jacket with a shaved*

head. When he introduced himself, he was very polite and well spoken. Richard had quite a high, rich singing voice and he picked the songs up very quickly; interestingly, he didn't mention much about his past and certainly nothing about working with Genesis. Of all the singers we auditioned, he was by far the best so we gave him the job. After he left we did all wonder where he'd been for the past ten years since he was a bit older than the rest of us (around 28 at the time) ... someone even jokingly suggested that he might have been in prison!

Little did they know...

We would meet at Mike's house and rehearse all the music Murray had written, just as we used to do when Ant wrote back in the days of Anon at Charterhouse. Like Ant, Murray could hear something once and then faithfully recreate it. His incredible talent was the rock that the band stood on. When we were ready, MC² did some gigs and a bit of recording in a makeshift studio Murray had set up in his bedroom. It was here that he wrote and we recorded a concept piece called *The Lion's Share*. It was a big stretch for me to master this complex vocal part but I relished the challenge.

Our biggest gig was at The Venue in Victoria, a sort of supper club-cum-theatre run by Richard Branson that was opposite the station. We opened for Spirit, the group who have recently been in the news for suing Led Zeppelin over 'Stairway To Heaven'. It was a big night for me so I felt very supported by my good friend Tony Levin, bass player from Peter Gabriel's band, turning up to cheer us on.

As much as I enjoyed working with MC² we had an intrinsic problem. Musically we were very comfortable but our age difference and my ten years' worth of experience in the music industry created a cultural gap between us. In some respects this might have been considered a good thing to have someone on board with my background, but I was the new recruit so it didn't really work out that way. Another problem was that we burst on to the scene in the middle of punk, or not long after, and bands like MC² were profoundly out of fashion. No record company would look at anything vaguely prog rock. Forget it. My tenure with them lasted a year or so and if nothing else, it helped get the singing bug out of my system. I left singing and it was only many years later that I discovered more satisfying ways of using my voice in the world.

During the time I was with MC^2, I was still living at Trellick Tower and, like many who harbour dreams of a performing career, was working as a minicab driver to make ends meet. After the Cohen tour I'd bought myself a white Volvo Estate, a real tank, and had joined a minicab company operating out of Great Titchfield Street in the West End. This was the centre of the rag trade. A good deal of our business was made up of journeys to and from the showrooms dotted up and down the street. Many of these outlets had sweatshops in either Hackney or Acton, so I spent quite a bit of my time hauling piles of dresses backwards and forwards between these two areas. They were all wholesale outlets so the staff from ladies fashion shops in towns like Tewkesbury or Kings Lynn would come up to London on a Friday morning, go around all the showrooms and buy a load of stock. This would be stuffed into black plastic bags and an estate car would then be called for to take them to Paddington or Euston or wherever. It was a good day's work.

The downside was that to drive a minicab requires an incredibly expensive insurance policy in case something bad happens to any of your passengers. What with the other costs of running a car in central London, I would typically work from Monday until lunchtime on Thursday to cover my expenses. Any money I made for myself came after that.

There were night drivers and day drivers. Night drivers were the cream of the crop; they tended to have much fancier cars since much of their work consisted of driving staff and punters home from restaurants, clubs and casinos at one or two o'clock in the morning. Many of these people lived way out in the suburbs so the night crew would take them. There would be no traffic, they'd receive a big fare and 15 minutes later they'd be back in the middle of London picking up someone else. The company only let the day drivers work on Friday nights, so that day I would start work a bit later, say 11 a.m., do the usual routine and then keep going until two or three the next morning. That ultra-long shift was when I made my week's profit.

I still remember the first day I became a driver. It was in the midst of a heat wave and my car didn't have air conditioning, a luxury in those days, so I was in my hot sweaty Volvo for hours on end. Of course there was no satnav back then so there was every cabbie's challenge of getting to know my way around the streets; one way this way for a block, then another way for another block... To find an address on Eastcastle Street, for example, was especially complicated because you had to do all the one-way wiggles and arrive on the right block facing in the right direction – an absolute nightmare. After that first day I was so exhausted that I headed home at 5.30 p.m. and went straight to bed. Learning this new job was shattering but I soon realised that mastering the one-way systems was the key and I quickly got on top of it. I had always admired London cab drivers but this experience deepened my respect for them.

The worst driving jobs were always the ones on account because the passengers never gave you a tip. Usually it was a group of well-dressed people from a glossy advertising agency going to a swanky restaurant in Charlotte Street. Having delivered them to their desired destination they would leap out, yell 'Thank you' and slam the door. The next week when the accounts were done and you saw what you'd made, it would be something like £1.75. Thanks very much.

What's more, I couldn't help but think there was an element of corruption in the minicab trade. Alan, the controller, definitely had his favourites. I'd hear him on the radio saying, '312 go down to High Street Kensington, Mr Jones, Heathrow Terminal 2 for cash', and I'd think, 'I've never been given a Heathrow for cash job. What's going on here?'

I used to have to wait up for maybe an hour in Foley Street, off Great Titchfield, until I finally made it to the top of the list according to the controller's random method of assigning jobs.

Then I'd get the message to go to wherever, probably close by and on account, do a job for £1.75 and find myself back at the bottom of the pile again.

To make things worse, the recession of 1980 arrived and the economy hit the skids. Our business did too. Lots of people were made redundant owing to 'poor trading conditions caused by the government's economic policies'; at least those were the grounds trotted out by employers. Plenty of people I knew would happily have pushed Thatcher off a cliff. I had been doing just about OK up to this point but suddenly I wasn't making any money. It simply wasn't working so I decided to switch to becoming a motorcycle messenger. My boss agreed and the next day I found myself at Pride & Clarke in Clerkenwell, an ancient and well-respected motorbike dealership. I bought myself a shiny blue Honda 250, the most powerful bike you could ride without a full licence in those days.

When arranging to pick up my new bike at the end of the week the guy at the shop asked me if I wanted to go on a safety course. I said yes and spent the following Saturday morning learning things that probably saved my life. Nowadays, when I see people on bikes doing daft things that suggest they clearly haven't been on the course, I worry for them. One simple lesson was that no matter how hot it is you should never ride your bike without gloves because if you come off, even though it might not be a serious tumble, your natural reaction is to put your hand out to break the fall. I've seen people with tarmac and grit driven into their palms because they didn't wear gloves.

Equipped with my new skills, the following Monday morning I was out on the streets of central London, earning my keep as a motorcycle messenger. In those days there weren't nearly as many of us as minicab drivers so I went from being a small fish in a big pond to being a tuna in a puddle. Suddenly I was Alan the controller's best mate and he would give me all the most lucrative jobs, thus proving my suspicions about his job distribution methods.

Funnily enough, no driver had ever switched from car to bike before and as time went on, motorcycle deliveries were in greater and greater demand. The costs of running a bike were a fraction of that of a car; there's no special insurance because you're not taking passengers, you're just delivering packages. It's zoom, zoom, zoom everywhere with no getting stuck in traffic. Bliss for a restless guy like me.

It was while I was a motorcycle messenger that I first met the woman who was to become my wife. Maggie Cole is a professional musician specialising in the harpsichord, piano and other keyboard instruments. If I hadn't decided to play hooky – as the Americans call it – one afternoon, we might never have got together.

One of my squatting mates, a photographer called Tony Sleep, was still living in the house in Freston Road, even though it was supposed to be all wound up. I had a bike job at 3.30 in the afternoon out to Acton, dropping off some swatches. After making the delivery I decided I couldn't be bothered to go all the way back into central London to get another job. 'I'll go and see Tony,' I thought, so I parked up and knocked on his door. I knew that he'd be in as he was often to be found working in his darkroom. A few minutes later, sitting over a cup of tea, the phone rang and even though it wasn't for me, that call would change my life.

Maggie and I were both single at the time and there seemed to be a general consensus among our mutual friends that we should meet. Matchmaking just wasn't our style so we had successfully resisted this idea. However, the Fates had a different notion. It was Maggie on the phone asking if she could drop by for a cup of tea. Ten minutes later we met. She liked my smile and with characteristic American forthrightness, asked me out that same evening. Like the typical shy public schoolboy that I was, I turned her down. I was completely freaked out.

As it happened, I was looking for a piano teacher at the time so I fixed up to have a lesson with her the following Saturday. The lessons continued for some months and began to include the odd coffee or movie date. Then one night she invited two old friends of mine over to dinner (the best bouillabaisse I had ever eaten) and I ended up not going home. From the moment that I met Maggie, I was captivated by her charm, intelligence and beauty. On top of that, she was an accomplished musician, although a very different one to what I was used to. That was over 35 years ago.

Our living situation was in many ways ideal. I had the centrally heated 27th floor in Trellick Tower and she had a flat in Arundel Gardens, right in the heart of Notting Hill with very little heating but an exquisite communal garden, part of the Landsdown Estate. We referred to them as our summer and winter palaces. These were very happy times as I had found someone with whom I was able to develop an intimate friendship. Finally, I was no longer on the road for ten months a year and a real and close relationship was possible. Among other things, Maggie opened up a whole new musical horizon for me. JS Bach has come to be my ultimate Desert Island composer.

But we were soon faced with a challenge. Maggie was already working as a musician, recording for Radio 3, giving concerts and teaching piano and harpsichord. The immigration authorities, however, had her registered as a music student. They also did not know that she was working as a waitress in a café in Westbourne Grove, the sort of place where customers ordered every variation of the Full English – eggs, bacon, beans and bubble, etc – and the waiting staff prided themselves on committing these orders to memory. After seven years in the UK, things were coming to a head as far as Maggie's immigration status was concerned. The moment came when, on returning from a trip to the US, an immigration official disappeared into the glass box with Maggie's passport for a long time. When he finally handed it back, it came with the strong but surprising advice that if she wanted to stay any longer, she should marry a Brit. It was too early in our relationship to contemplate the idea but we felt deeply committed to each other and weren't willing to allow the Home Office to split us up.

In the end, we decided we had to solve the immigration problem and married in secret. We booked a date at the Chelsea Town Hall on the Kings Road and invited a Scottish friend who had also married an American woman (they're still together) to come along and be our witness. Somehow we forgot that we actually needed two.

It was November 1981. We arrived at Chelsea Register Office for our 11 a.m. appointment and realised we were a witness short.

We spotted a guy sitting on a bench outside the Town Hall and went up and asked him if he had 20 minutes to spare. 'Yes,' he said. 'I've just hitchhiked from Aberdeen to meet my girlfriend here and I'm early. I've been working on the oil rigs.' He was an oil geologist, specifically what is known as a mud logger. He thought that acting as our witness would add a little spice to the journal he was keeping. We dragged him in and that was that, just the four of us. A severe woman with dead white pancake make-up and a black dress with white trim introduced herself as the registrar. We stood there quaking as she fired penetrating questions at us. 'What, no ring?' 'You only met the couple five minutes ago?' It was plainly obvious what was going on but there was nothing to stop the ceremony from proceeding.

So we got married. Maggie got the requisite stamp in her passport and a motorcycle messenger for a husband. She had faith that my working life would take a more interesting and fruitful turn and she was right.

Chapter 18

THE REUNION

At one point, Peter forgot some of his words.
He didn't have to worry; the entire audience sang
along for him and they were word perfect. I was at the
mixing desk, so deeply moved that I couldn't join in.

Being a motorcycle messenger was all very well but it was hardly
a career that would ultimately satisfy me. It could be argued that
tour-managing rock bands had potential for wider expansion;
several I knew had ended up as managers of successful bands or
now ran lighting companies or designed stages. A few, not many
but a significant number, had become richer than the bands whose
amps they had once lugged around the world but I was stymied by
having started out in the game as a friend and not a hired hand.
With both Genesis and Peter, I wanted to be their friend and to
work for them, until I came to realise that I couldn't do both. The
reality was that I didn't much enjoy tour managing anyone else. It
was a Catch 22 and when I opted to get out of the touring game
completely I cast a wary eye out for an opportunity that suited
my experience, temperament and interests. Fortunately, it wasn't
long in coming.

Around the time I got together with Maggie, I was again
involved with the EST organisation and through it met a
proud Welshman called Dyfrig Hughes who worked as an

oceanographer for the Ministry of Agriculture & Fisheries in Norwich and was also involved with Friends of the Earth. As a keen environmentalist, he decided to switch from being involved with measuring the dwindling shoals of fish on the Dogger Bank to working in the field of energy and the built environment. When I met him he was working at the Polytechnic of Central London (now the University of Westminster) opposite Madame Tussauds. His outfit was called the Built Environment Research Group (BERG), set up and run by a man called Ray Maw.

Ray was a genuine visionary whose work and ideas presaged the UK environmental movement, especially in relation to the energy efficiency of buildings. He was very good at attracting funding and Dyfrig was doing a research project on solar energy, then in its infancy. We met at an EST seminar in 1981 when I was between jobs. The people at BERG wanted to set up a demonstration centre for this new technology in a row of railway arches next to St Pancras Station, on the corner of what is now the British Library. At the time the land was used as a car park, leased to NCP, but the arches were redundant so Ray rented them for next to nothing. Dyfrig asked me whether I had ever organised exhibitions. 'Well no,' I told him, 'but I was a road manager, so in a way I put on an exhibition every night, a mobile exhibition.' The thing about being a road manager is that it is excellent training for managing just about anything, however large or small. I had a hunch that there was an opportunity for me here and initially began by organising the refurbishment of those arches.

This was the era of Ken Livingstone's Greater London Council (GLC). Thatcher was Prime Minister. Across the river from the Houses of Parliament stood County Hall where Livingstone had put up a huge sign with the number of unemployed people written on it, right across from Parliament, to remind the Tories of the effect that their economic policies were having in London. Since companies were leaving the capital in droves to save costs, Ken was keen on schemes that would foster employment and for this reason he supported initiatives like BERG.

Ken and his team believed quite rightly that new technology could spawn businesses and create employment, so they set up various technology networks, one of which was the London Energy and Employment Network. We applied for a grant to turn the railways arches into offices and much to our delight the application was approved. I was brought in as building manager, organising the facility, commissioning contractors and getting the building work done. It wasn't long before I started to get extremely interested in what they were about, which was essentially investigating and then promoting the concept of energy efficiency in housing. They were 20 to 25 years ahead of their time. Thousands of people have solar energy in their houses now but back then it was an unknown field and also prohibitively expensive. Solar panels on roofs were as futuristic back then as home computers.

We soon realised that the energy efficiency of the country's housing stock was appalling, as anybody who lives in a house in England that is older than 30 or 40 years will know. Much of the country's housing was built before the First World War, after which there was a big building boom between the wars with hundreds of thousands of dwellings built in the 30s but none constructed with any thought given to energy efficiency. The whole issue was in its infancy and we were quick to realise that there was a massive job to be done to bring it up to something resembling contemporary standards. Once again, I found myself on the ground floor of a new and exciting enterprise. At this point there were no more than a dozen people in this field and we all knew one another.

Using the money from the GLC, we set up a company with two branches: a charitable and a commercial side. I was a director and shareholder of the commercial wing, which was called OPTIMA Energy and we became quite successful. In fact, after a few years we were turning over a million pounds a year and employing 30 people.

The principal source of our income was derived from developing a consultancy service for local authorities. In those days local councils had big housing stocks and the Department for Environment was putting pressure on them to raise the energy efficiency of their properties. It was clear to everyone that those who lived in local authority houses were families on low incomes and the last thing they needed was a huge energy bill. Our role was to advise the local authorities about energy efficiency when they were building new houses and also when old ones came up for refurbishment.

Dyfrig was one of the first people to realise the potential of using computer software to assess the energy efficiency of housing and what could be done to improve it. My speciality became the development and running of training courses. In one form or another, these same courses are still being given today and have been delivered to thousands of people, all of them providing advice to householders about improving the energy efficiency of their houses. The students typically worked for local authorities, housing associations, utility companies and government departments. Increasingly, towards the end they worked for organisations like ours of which OPTIMA was the first. In addition to being passionate about the subject matter, delivering the courses satisfied the performer in me. Of course, I gained a lot of knowledge in the process. I became a recognised national expert in the field, appearing on TV and radio, talking about energy in housing stock. ITV even got me to do a show in which they took pictures of famous people's houses but didn't tell me to whom they belonged. I was to look at the pictures and say what was wrong with them, then would come the punch line: well, that's Paul McCartney's house or whatever. It was a bit of a nasty angle and I didn't really like playing along.

In the year 2000, OPTIMA merged with another company called National Energy Services (NES), based in Milton Keynes. By now NES were the leading organisation writing software that assessed the energy efficiency of houses and we'd been closely associated with them because their staff learned much of what they knew from our courses. Soon after the merger, the European Union announced their intention to bring in a directive known as the Energy Performance of Buildings Directive, which decreed that in all EU countries, when a building was newly built or rented to a new tenant, or if it were bought and sold, it needed to have an Energy Performance Certificate, an EPC as it came to be known.

Nowadays it's familiar to anybody buying or selling a house, but at the beginning NES was in pole position as one of the leading organisations taking this forward. We were there from the start. I set up and ran the training and for six years I worked very hard coaching Domestic Energy Assessors. The EPC is now an established part of an estate agency's details when a house changes hands.

In 2010, just as the EPC rule was implemented, the housing market collapsed and the volume of homes changing hands dropped dramatically. The upshot was that many of the people I had trained became unemployed. It took between six and eight months to train as a DEA and now there was only work for about half of them. I found this sad and demoralising and difficult to separate from my personal story. After all, OPTIMA had provided me with a good living from the time I stopped working as a tour manager through the rest of my working life.

That life wasn't entirely bereft of celebrity company. One day, on my way to the dentist as it happens, my phone rang. 'Hello, it's Ken Livingstone here. Are you the guy who does the energy surveys?' I thought it was a friend taking the piss but it was in fact Ken, a man I admired greatly and to whom I had good reason to be grateful for setting me up in the energy business in the first place. At the time, Ken was up for election as mayor of London against Boris Johnson, which he regrettably lost, and prior to the election he wanted to make sure his house was up to scratch energy-wise. The right-wing press, always willing to try and exploit any perceived weak spots in Ken, would happily have branded him a hypocrite if his own house wasn't up to standard. So there we were, Ken and I, sitting at his kitchen table sorting out a plan of action. At the end of our meeting, I told him, 'I wouldn't be here now if it weren't for you.' What a pleasure it was, after all those years, to thank him for the money the GLC put up to get our company started. Dozens of people had built careers from what we did – and it was all thanks to him. He really appreciated my saying this. So don't believe all that you may read about 'Red Ken'. He's one of the good guys!

It probably goes without saying that during the time I spent at OPTIMA and NES I kept up my friendships with the guys in Genesis. To their fans they were a supergroup but to me they were still among the oldest mates I had and although I was no longer on their payroll, I listened avidly to their ever more commercial music and went along to concerts, each one bigger than the last. I stood on the sidelines and watched in wonder as they grew into one of the biggest bands in the world. They were now down to just three of the originals, Tony, Mike and Phil, augmented on tour by Chester Thompson on drums and Daryl Stuermer on guitars. Meanwhile Peter Gabriel became just as successful in his own right, that rare combination of authentic artistry and popular acclaim pushing him ever upwards after the enormous success of *So* in 1986. Finally, it seemed, he'd been persuaded to give his albums proper titles other than simply *Peter Gabriel*, but even then he perversely chose the shortest names he could, continuing in this way with *Us*, *Up* and *OVO*.

Peter had long been entranced and influenced by music from different cultures all over the world. Increasingly, he collaborated with musicians from Africa, the Middle East and South East Asia, becoming an important champion of what is now referred to as 'world music'. His sympathy for the plight of those living under the yoke of repressive regimes in these regions was best reflected in 'Biko', a track on his third ('Melt') album; this haunting song was about Steven Biko, a black South African anti-apartheid activist who was murdered by South African police while under arrest in 1977. Peter also took part alongside Bruce Springsteen, Sting, Tracy Chapman and Youssou N'Dour in the Human Rights Now! tour that traversed the globe in 1988, distinguishing himself with his persuasive oratory during press conferences along the way.

Nowhere did Peter wear his heart on his sleeve with more conviction than in creating and promoting WOMAD (the World of Music and Dance), a festival of world music that received massive critical acclaim and almost bankrupted him when he launched it in 1982. That first festival took place in the West Country, outside Shepton Mallet in the same field where Led Zeppelin stormed the second Bath Festival in 1970. The whole event presented huge challenges: the audience were in raptures but ticket sales were dire, the weather was bleak, the BBC pulled out of a promised telecast and a train strike kept people away. Limitations imposed by the local authority meant the most popular acts were restricted in where they could play and, of course, all these world performers weren't exactly local, so airfares from all over the globe fell to Peter to pay.

It's no secret that Peter and Jill received death threats from people to whom they owed money. 'It became a nightmare experience when we realised there was no way we were getting the ticket sales to cover our costs,' Peter told the *Guardian* in 2012. 'The debts were way above what I could manage but people saw me as the only fat cat worth squeezing so I got a lot of nasty phone calls and a death threat.'

It wasn't long before Peter's dilemma came to the attention of the rest of the band and in an extraordinary act of generosity, Tony Smith suggested that they rally round to help their friend, staging a one-off reunion gig with Peter on vocals to raise the money needed to pay all the creditors. It happened on October 2nd 1982 at the Milton Keynes Bowl, a big capacity stadium that was quickly sold out. It's the only reunion gig Genesis has ever done with Peter and I doubt that there will ever be another.

The decision to play the reunion show is a reflection of something I've always loved about Genesis. All five members of the original band – and I can even include Ant in this, so that brings it to six – remain very close, still the best of friends. They might not play together any longer but the camaraderie is still there. Other bands of their era or status have split up or fragmented in ways that leave certain members continuing in a poor imitation of the original group and others left by the wayside. Mike Rutherford agrees:

When I think about it, I'm conscious of how we're really good friends in spite of it all. First and foremost I put that down to

the fact that we never argued about money. What I've observed
with other bands is that people get too big for their boots and
they don't want anyone to push them around. But if you've been
at school with someone and you go back that far, it's harder to
play those destructive games.

The day of the reunion gig also happened to be Mike's birthday.
It was one of those days, rare even for England, when you get
up in the morning to find that it's raining, it rains all day and
when you go to bed it's still raining – not great for an outdoor
concert in chilly early October. But it would have taken more
than atrocious weather to keep Genesis fans away, especially with
that weird chap who dressed up like a sunflower back on vocals.
Everybody showed up in their wellington boots and waterproofs.
Genesis were about to start a European tour and the Showco
sound and light crew were already in the UK setting up, so the
machinery was up and running. There were the five originals on
stage with Daryl and Chester to beef up the sound. At one point,
Peter forgot some of his words. He didn't have to worry; the entire
audience sang along for him and they were word perfect. I was at
the mixing desk, so deeply moved that I couldn't join in. People
still talk about that day as one of those rare and special events.
'I was there,' they tell the next generations of Genesis fans.

Armando Gallo, Italian photojournalist, mad Genesis fan
from the beginning and the first person to write a book about
the group, was in London at the time, as were the band Toto, big
Genesis fans and friends of Armando. 'Can we go?' they asked
him. Of course they could. I remember being backstage in the
car park when two black limos arrived and parked up. Out got
all these very groovy looking people, including Armando who
introduced me to everyone. Among the party was the actress
Rosanna Arquette, girlfriend of Toto's keyboard player Steve
Porcaro, dressed top to toe in black leather – very alluring, very
beautiful and, as it happened, very distracting for Peter.

When a band plays a big stadium show they have two choices at
the end. One is to do a runner where they drop everything, jump

in their cars and leave while the audience are still screaming for more. The other option is to wait, essentially to throw a backstage party, linger for an hour-and-a-half while the traffic eases off and then make their getaway. Clearly on this occasion it would have been inappropriate to do a runner, so there was a big backstage party – lots of backslapping, toasting Mike's birthday, the whole gang back together. In the midst of all this Peter was introduced to Rosanna and he fell for her big time.

In one great swish, the winds of fate paid off Peter's debt and changed the course of his life. It was some time before Peter and Rosanna got together (in the intervening years she had a brief marriage to James Newton Howard, the renowned film composer) but Peter pursued her from the moment they met at the reunion show and after a great deal of soul-searching and distress for all concerned, his marriage with Jill finally came to an end. Rosanna and Peter stayed together for four or five years but a clash of careers – she was on the cusp of making it big in *Desperately Seeking Susan*, co-starring alongside Madonna – and the challenge of a long-distance relationship proved too much for both of them.

I am well aware that a book such as this should include some juicy revelations regarding the private lives of my well-known friends. I hope that Peter will forgive me for saying that, having not sown the proverbial wild oats in his youth, he now made up for lost time. He proceeded to step out with Marie Helvin, Naomi Campbell and Sinead O'Connor among others.

I have it on Peter's authority that Sinead lived up to her tempestuous reputation. One day when the two of them were staying in a New York hotel an argument developed about, well, let's call it Peter's roving eye, which led to Sinead picking up his Filofax address book and throwing it into the bathtub where he was relaxing at the time. It had all his girlfriends' phone numbers in it and she wanted to wash them all away. Some time later, I was with Peter and noticed that his Filofax was all blotched and runny. 'Sinead,' he said, rolling his eyes before recounting the story.

Many infer from the Godley and Creme video for 'Don't Give Up' that Kate Bush was among Peter's conquests but this wasn't so.

Peter had become the agent for a groundbreaking synthesiser, an Australian invention called the Fairlight, and had set up a company with his cousin, Stephen Paine, to market it. Not surprisingly, they went to the top in terms of clients as the instruments cost £30,000 a piece. Abba, Led Zeppelin and Pink Floyd all bought one, as did Kate Bush which is how they met. A deep musical relationship based upon mutual respect ensued and it remained purely platonic.

Among those who bought a Fairlight was Stevie Wonder who immediately began using it on stage. I remember Stevie playing Wembley and wanting to demonstrate his famous sense of humour with this new toy. Having learned how to sample the sound of a dog barking, Mr Wonder called out, 'Where's the guy from Fairlight?' whereupon Stephen jumped on stage and sat next to him. We soon heard 'Woof, woof, woof...' to the tune of 'Jingle Bells'. Everybody was laughing and applauding.

All of this brings me just about to where I am now. But what became of the others in my story? My parents lived long and happy lives, eventually retiring to Chichester, which they chose because of their love of the theatre and being churchy types, the cathedral, where they became volunteer guides. They wanted a house with a view of the cathedral spire and, looking around one day, found a street in central Chichester close to the north side of the cathedral. It was a Sunday afternoon and my dad knocked on the door of a house on this street, took off his hat and in his characteristically gracious manner asked if by any chance the occupants knew of any houses on the street that were on the market. These same people told him they were about to put their house up for sale and my parents bought it there and then, thus avoiding agent's fees. He always was a lucky bugger in the property game, my old man.

My father died in 1995, my mother three years later, a few weeks before her 90th birthday. The last time I visited my father he knew he was dying. From his deathbed he apologised for not supporting me more with my own musical aspirations. He said, 'I didn't understand your passion and for that, I am sorry'. Both my parents adored Maggie and her music, which seemed to create a bridge between them and me.

My eldest sister Moira married the clever scientist who fixed me up with my first stereo system all those years ago and he is now a webmaster. Moira has an incredible gift for sewing crafts and the two of them are at the centre of their village community. They have two children and four grandchildren. My middle sister Kate lives in Devizes and is now retired from special needs teaching. It's always a joy to go shopping with her in Devizes because just about every other person we come across was taught by her and greets her with great fondness. She has two children and two grandchildren.

Nowadays I've come a full circle and I am Maggie's driver, tour manager and 'perse'. I can't help but help out because I can see things that need doing and I do them, just like I did with Genesis in Christmas Cottage, on my tours with them and with Peter. It's instinct I guess – checking access, power points, sight lines, all the same things that artists need, whether it be a mega selling rock band or a solo harpsichordist. Not that Maggie is always solo. She does around 75 gigs a year, so what with preparing for them she's busy a lot of the time, far busier than I am. When she's not actually gigging she is teaching. She's a professor at the Guildhall of the forte piano, an early version of the piano, which is the missing link between harpsichord and the modern piano. She has private students who come to the house, has released numerous CDs and also performs with two trios, one in the UK and one in Israel. In addition, she has duet partners and accompanies singers. All of this has opened me up to other types of music; on top of JS Bach, I love all the material she plays, which runs from Elizabethan music to the 20th century.

In my retirement I have found a new way of sharing my love of all things musical. I've started an internet radio station called Radio Rich Pickings (search Facebook) for which I get to roam far and wide, choosing music from the enormous range that I have come to love over my rich and varied life. I notice that the radio has proved to be the latest outlet for that voice of mine, the same voice that found expression as a rock singer in my early years and later as a trainer. Maggie and I cherish our friendships with Tony, Mike, Phil, Ant, Steve and Peter, my good old mates with whom I shared so many adventures.

So, dear reader, we've come to the end of my tale. As I said at the very beginning, I embarked on this project with the intention of telling my part of the Genesis story but as the process unfolded, a different perspective emerged. Being born into 1950s England was an amazing piece of luck. The Second World War was over, a period of prosperity was beginning and the threat of global nuclear war ironically ensured an unprecedented era of peace. My generation did not have to go to war, enjoyed free university education, jobs, affordable jet travel and a sense of limitless possibilities. On top of all this, we witnessed the greatest explosion of popular music the world has ever seen and I was blessed to be at the centre of it all. As a good friend said to me in the mid-70s: 'Richard, you live a charmed life.' I have been very fortunate and for that I am deeply grateful.

Appendix

AN INTERVIEW WITH STEVE HACKETT

As is clear from the text of this book, I conducted new interviews with Mike Rutherford, Tony Banks, Phil Collins and Steve Hackett to enhance it and, perhaps, clarify points I make about the early years of Genesis when I was working with them. By and large, Mike, Tony and Phil restricted their remarks to the group as it was until Peter Gabriel chose to leave. Steve, on the other hand, broadened his remarks to offer a more rounded picture, to talk about the band's working methods and to touch on the reasons for his own departure. Since I had also left by this time it didn't obviously fit into the main story, but I felt that what he said was significant and, more importantly, would be of interest to Genesis fans.

So here is the interview, more or less verbatim with a few interjections from me.

SH: I'm very proud of my contribution to Genesis. It wasn't an easy team. I don't think it was easy to be a five-man active team. I know that Pete was often at odds with Tony and Mike. Obviously, politically I found that Mike would always back Tony. He knew how to pull everyone's strings.

RPM: Yes, and most people think it was Tony.

SH: But the prime mover, initially, in terms of galvanising interest in the band was Pete. If he was late to a rehearsal it was because he was on the phone hustling. He was a prime hustler. Later on,

221

I thought, 'I've got to be the band's publicist.' No one realises this, but the nights that I spent up and down Wardour Street watering holes and the Speakeasy, talking the press into doing stuff for us, being the man on the spot...

RPM: I didn't know that.

SH: I took on that role. I wanted to be someone who had an overview because I realised that within the band you couldn't always get a look in with the song writing. Basically Tony wanted to do it all but only allowed others in when he wanted it.

RPM: Are you saying he was always like that? I know that's basically why you left.

SH: No, the reason why I left – and that's another story – was because new boy Hackett had a hit on his own which no one was expecting. No one was expecting my album to be any good. That was *Acolyte*, and suddenly I was able to count Pete and his wife Jill among my fans. They liked it very much. He'd already left of course, and Tony said to me, 'If you can write a bass line like that you're doing alright.' But we used part of something on that album that Mike had offered to the band, a tune called 'Shadow Of the Hierophant', and I still play this live. It brings the house down. He [Mike] presented it around the time of *Foxtrot* but it had been rejected. I thought it was marvellous. 'Why are we rejecting that?' It had to be political. So I said to him, three years later, 'cos he was helping me make that album, I said, 'Do you mind if we use that? It doesn't look like the band is going to use it.' He said, 'No, I don't think they will, so OK fine.' So we did it and afterwards Tony said to me, 'You know we could have used that for Genesis.' That was three years later.

It was the same thing with the guitar riff in 'I Know What I Like'. I presented it at the time of *Foxtrot* and Mike said, 'Sounds too much like George Harrison. We can't use that. We can't sound like The Beatles.' The following year, I'm still doing it, still jamming away on it, Phil and myself, and then the band join in, it gets written, goes on *Selling England*, our first hit single. The moral is 'Stick to your guns with things that get rejected.' Even Pink Floyd were overlooking things. The thing that became 'Us and Them' had been used as part of the soundtrack to *Obscured By Clouds*. A good idea is always worth preserving. It's a little bit like the *I Ching*, if I may quote from it... the bit devoted to 'work on that which has been spoiled' is perfect for music because if you've done a song that didn't quite take off or nobody liked it, you can always do it again because its time might be tomorrow if it's not today.

RPM: The concept of time is so fickle, so subject to other things.

SH: The song that was the huge hit in the *Robin Hood* movie, written by Michael Kamen... I asked him when he wrote that and he said, 'Twenty years earlier'. Twenty years of people turning that down. So don't give up, to quote another song.

After a discussion of the reasons for Peter leaving Genesis, Steve spoke more about The Lamb.

SH: I've always tried to invent the term for what we were doing then and I'm still doing now, which is collision. Fusion says it to a certain extent, progression says it to a certain extent but I think, with all these descriptions of musical genres, no matter whether the term is apart or not, people will always think that progressive means Mellotron, Hammond, long-form punctuation driven songs, unusual chords, impenetrable, all the reasons why people hate it. It doesn't have to be. It can be romantic. It's got as much to do with Jimmy Webb, as much to do with 'MacArthur Park' as anything else. Long-form pop is prog. It's a catch-all really.

I don't have any rules. I don't mind if a song is three notes long or if it's a 23- or 26-minute epic like 'Supper's Ready'. It doesn't matter. If you retain the audience's interest that's fine. Why argue with the length of the song?

RPM: Mike said something... about the whole long/short thing: 'Good short songs are harder to write.'

SH: Yes, the epitome of the form is 'Eleanor Rigby'. The life and death of an old woman, compassionate, to step outside yourself and to step outside the box.

Luckily I worked with a guy called Roger King and for me he's a combination of Geoff Emerick and George Martin all rolled into one. And Keith Emerson. He combines all of those schooled qualities. I'm the great illogical dreamer. I don't have any rules. I don't have any schooling. I've got immense respect for orchestras.

RPM: My only regret about this whole thing is that we didn't have the equipment that exists today.

SH: Oh yes, there's no tyranny of volume. If I want feedback, the guitar will produce feedback itself. Some of the most screaming solos I record these days I can record anywhere. People ask, 'Why are you recording in the living room?' Because I can. This is a conversation I had with Chris Squire [co-founder and bassist of Yes]. Sometimes we only go on location to make it look good for the cameras.

RPM: So looking back...

SH: It's lovely talking to you like this because we can sit back with all the detritus, all the dead bodies and say... [what we want]. I wouldn't say boo to a goose in those days. I was so shy. I was completely introverted but determined that I was going to get somewhere, that this band was going to get somewhere. I thought the best way to do it was... if someone is doing anything interesting in a corner, i.e. Tony or Mike or Phil, I would immediately say, 'That's good. I think we should use that,' and then someone would say, 'Oh, we can't use that because we used it on an earlier tune.' And I'd say, 'Did you record that tune?' 'No.' 'Well, why don't we use it?'

RPM: So it's not just public schoolboys that don't say the important shit. I just thought that the band was really good and the world needed to hear them and I would do anything to make it work.

SH: And the band was getting better all the time. We weren't perfect. It was a slow growth [to] how professional it became. It was extraordinary.

RPM: Phil said in hindsight that Mike and Tony were pretty uncompromising. Peter was saying he needed some time out to work with William Friedkin and their response was, 'You're in or out,' forcing his hand. Phil said that was a mistake.

SH: I'm glad you're saying that. You can paraphrase that as if it was my answer too. It's the same thing when I did *Acolyte* and it became a success. They got very pissed off and said you can't have a parallel solo career while you're in the band. Of course, Phil went and did that, and so did Mike and then Tony.

RPM: Tony wasn't successful.

SH: At that time it was considered very uncool to do that. Never mind the fact that Phil had a whole band of his own. I could have said, 'I could have had a band of my own and called it, I dunno, the Fabulous Dooberies,' but I shouldn't have listened. It made for a very difficult atmosphere because I realised there was no guarantee that any idea I came up with would get used, so when two people in the band turn around and say to you, 'We don't think you're giving everything to the band, Steve,' well, what's the band giving me? That's the thing. Are you prepared to listen to my ideas? Do you like songs like 'Blood On the Rooftops', like 'Los Endos', like 'The Dance Of the Volcano'? I'd be quite happy if someone criticised 'Ghostliners' because we never did it with the band. We did it three times in Italy, we only played it live.

RPM: It's such a good song.

SH: It goes places. There are two schools of thought. I know in Phil's book he criticises that and says that about songs like 'Across the River' but it's missing the point. It's a song that goes through many changes. It's prototype prog and we didn't know that what we were doing was prototype prog because there hadn't been a blueprint for it. It was a long tune.

I'd seen King Crimson live and sometimes they'd do a long tune, 15 minutes, and sometimes they'd change it and stick 'The Young Ones' in the middle of it and go off and do that. But they'd link things. Ian McDonald told me later that they did it with a system of cues. We'd let it deteriorate until someone would play something that was a cue. 'Ahhh', I thought it was telepathy, but someone would play a couple of notes. You can do so much with that, a system of signals; you have to keep your ears open of course. I do that as a bandleader now... it's all arranged.

Eventually Genesis were doing that within *The Lamb*. I think so many [live] versions of *The Lamb* were better than the way it was on the record.... 'The Waiting Room', which we used to call the 'Evil Jam'. No one had any idea that Miles Davis had done *Live-Evil* but we were subscribing to the same notion.

RPM: It seems to me that the best way to work was when we were on the road, to write a song, play it live, hone it and then record it.

SH: It's a luxury. Once you get on the treadmill of doing album–tour, album–tour, you no longer have that. It's something that bands often achieve in their formative stages.

RPM: That's why the first album is often so good. And the second one is not so good because they get successful and they get on to the treadmill, as you call it.

SH: In hindsight, *Foxtrot* is at least as strong as *Nursery Cryme*... *Nursery Cryme* has some marvellous moments on it. I think all the Genesis albums have marvellous moments, both before me, during me and after me. I'm generous enough to say that.

There'll always be something that's brilliant – drumming, production techniques – and that's the thing about Genesis... something for everybody.

RPM: It seems so... 400 million albums later. Whatever it was.

SH: The truth is, no act knows exactly how many albums they've sold because, to quote a lawyer I was talking to, this industry is an invitation to steal.

MY BOOK OF GENESIS

INDEX

10cc 166

Abba 218
Action, The 36
Adey, Les 134-136
Alexander, John 35, 54
Anderson, Ian 127
Anderson, Jon 92
Anon (group) 33, 35, 41
Anthony, John 73-74, 76, 80, 103
Arquette, Rosanna 216-217
Austin Hippy Blues Band, The 48

Banks, Margaret (née McBain) 76, 99, 107, 115, 127, 135, 145, 150, 171
Banks, Tony 61, 64, 66, 73, 74, 75, 79, 81-82, 86, 90, 96, 99, 105, 112, 122, 124, 128, 130, 133, 143, 148, 169, 212, 217; and The Garden Wall 37-38; as keyboard player 71, 85, 94; at Charterhouse 30; at Christmas Cottage 69, 70; formation of Genesis 54; on Genesis's musical style 109-110; on Peter Gabriel leaving Genesis 145-146, 148; pragmatism 82, 106, 126-127, 150-151; recording *From Genesis To Revelation* 54
Barclay James Harvest 95
Bayeté (aka Cochran, Todd) 162, 171
Beach Boys, The 125, 126, 139
Beatles, The 9, 25, 30, 35, 39, 103, 128, 197, 222

Beck, Jeff 63
Beck, Roscoe 197
Bee Gees, The 54
Berger, Hugh 133
Berlins, Jeff 192
Bicknell, Markus 72, 74
'Biko' 214
Biko, Steve 214
Bilezikjian, John 197
Black Oak Arkansas 137-138
Black, Philip 44, 133
Bluesology 37
Boff, Regis 123, 147
Bogart, Neil 121, 123, 125
Bonnet, Graham 150
Bonzo Dog Doo-Dah Band, The 80
Bowie, David 96, 163
Brand X 177-181, 183
Briggs, Chris 80, 96
Brooks, Elkie 125
Bruford, Bill 92, 151, 192
Burns, John 110, 143
Bush, Kate 217-218

Caddy, Peter 132
Campbell, Naomi 217
Caravan 95
Caryl, Ronnie 85
Chapman, Tracy 214
Charlesworth, Chris 15, 77
Charr, 'Hacker' 34

Chicago 174, 180
Clapton, Eric 42
Cobham, Billy 92
Cohen, Leonard 196-199, 201
Cole, Maggie (aka Macphail, Maggie) 59, 164, 177, 192, 196, 201, 206-208, 209, 218-219
Coleman, Mick 35
Collins, Phil 87, 89, 90, 93, 94, 97, 99, 100, 101, 102, 107, 112, 128-129, 212, 217; and Brand X 177-181; autobiography (*Not Dead Yet*) 84-85, 131; becomes Genesis's singer 150-152; Genesis audition 83-84; on Peter Gabriel leaving Genesis 145; personality 85, 98; workaholic tendencies 178
Colson, Gail 51, 74, 75, 79, 80, 86, 87, 93, 104, 161, 171, 175, 177, 183, 196, 197
Colson, Glen 74
Conroy, Paul 80, 96, 112
Cooper, Alice 156, 162
Corey-Wright, Anthony 45
Corey-Wright, David 45
Corey-Wright, Jane 45
Cowe, Betsy (aka Gibson, Betsy) 100-101, 105, 149
Cowe, Simon 100
'Crackie' 106
Crosby, Stills, Nash & Young 84
Cutler, Horace 157

Dandy, Jim 137, 152
Davidson, Paul 112
Davies, Miranda 76, 133
Deacon, John 96
Dennard, Kenwood 178-180, 183
'Don't Give Up' 217
Doobie Brothers, The 182
Dunbar, Sly & Shakespeare, Robbie 190

Edwards, Gareth 44
Emerson, Keith 80, 108, 224
Emerson, Lake & Palmer 80, 106, 108
Enthoven, David 93

Erhard, Werner 149
Evans, Guy 106
Ezrin, Bob 156

Faithfull, Marianne 36
Farrell, Mike 134, 135, 179
Fast, Larry 156, 162, 168, 171
Firth, John 62
Flaming Youth 83, 85, 103
Fleming, Ian 158
'Fly On a Windshield' 146
Flynn, Roy 103
Ford, Geoffrey 37, 39
'Fountains Of Salmacis' 114
Foxtrot 83, 107, 108, 109, 110, 111, 119, 126, 127, 130, 222, 226
Fraser, Andy 108
Fraser, Dick 179
Free 108
Friedkin, William 127, 146, 225
Fripp, Robert 93-94, 155, 156, 162-163
From Genesis To Revelation 55, 63, 66

Gabriel, Anna Marie 144
Gabriel, Irene 78, 144
Gabriel, Jill (née Moore) 38, 64, 70, 75, 76, 99, 103, 126, 143-146, 149, 164, 179, 184, 215, 217, 222
Gabriel, Melanie 155
Gabriel, Peter 40, 62, 65, 66, 73, 74, 75-76, 77, 79, 82, 90, 95-97, 101, 102, 105, 112, 125, 126, 130, 147, 148, 150, 169, 173, 179, 179, 181, 190, 191, 195, 207, 212, 215, 217; and The Garden Wall 38-39; and WOMAD 214-215; at Charterhouse 30, 38; at Christmas Cottage 68, 72; formation of Genesis 54; issues re family responsibilities 144-145; leaves Genesis 129, 148-149; personality 160-161; recording *From Genesis To Revelation* 54; recording *The Lamb Lies Down On Broadway* 144-147; solo touring 160-165, 167-168; stagemanship 66,

94, 126-127, 168-169; vacillation 159-160; vivid imagination 38-39
Gabriel, Ralph 64, 78
Gallo, Armando 113, 216
Garden Wall, The (group) 37-39
Gaydon, Johnny 93
Gaye, Marvin 160
Genesis 55, 61, 63, 65, 72, 86, 127, 135, 139, 179, 181, 195, 196, 207; American tours 121-125, 135-136, 147-148; as four-piece after Ant's departure 85-86; at Christmas Cottage 68-72; become managed by Tony Smith 132; early Italian tours 109, 111-115; festival appearances 125-126; finances 78, 83, 99-101; formation 41, 53; musical development 66; musical style 93-94. 103, 108; on the road 91-92, 94-97, 102, 105-108; recording *Nursery Cryme* 102-103; recording *The Lamb Lies Down On Broadway* 144-147; recording *Trespass* 80; signs to Charisma Records 76; 1982 reunion show 215-217
Genesis Live 119, 127
Gibb, Robin 54
Ginn, Bill 197
Glover, Helen 44
Goldfinger, Ernö 117, 158
Goldsmith, Harvey 194
Goldsworthy, Anne 78
Goodgold, Ed 121, 123, 125
Goodhew, Duncan 44
Goodsall, John 178
Grade, Lady Kathy 133
Grade, Lew 44, 133

Hackett, Ellen 145
Hackett, Oliver 145
Hackett, Steve 69, 90, 91, 97, 99, 100, 106, 129; interview 221-227; joins Genesis/early gigs 86, 88-89; on Genesis's popularity in Italy 114; on Peter Gabriel leaving Genesis 148
Hakopian, Raff 197
Hammill, Peter 179, 180, 183-191

Harrington, Tony 136
Harris, Mike 201
Hatfield & the North 151, 192
Helvin, Marie 217
Hendrix, Jimi 37
'Here Comes the Flood' 155
Howard, James Newton 217
Howard, Ken & Blakely, Alan 83
Hughes, Dyfrig 209, 210, 212
Hunter, Ian 73
Hunter, Steve 156, 162

Ingerson, Cass 158

Jackson, Dave 106
Jagger, Mick 23, 25, 29, 35, 41, 43, 107, 190
Janessa 149, 158, 162, 180
Jeff Beck Group, The 37
Jenson, Kid 99
Jethro Tull 106, 127
Job, Charlotte 28, 42
Job, Crispin 28
Job, Rivers 9, 27-31, 35, 37, 39, 41, 42, 50, 133
Job, Rowan Maitland Alexandra 31
John, Elton 37
Jones, Brian 43
Jones, Percy 178, 180, 183

Keef Hartley Band, The 96
King Crimson 93, 151, 156, 163, 164, 179, 192, 226
King, Jonathan 54, 67, 79
King, Reg 78-79, 94, 97, 111
King, Terry 76, 80, 91, 97
'Knife, The' 71, 128
Kirk, Rahsaan Roland 195
Kossoff, Paul 108

Lamb Lies Down On Broadway, The 127, 141, 143, 144-148, 153, 223, 226
Langham, Chris 75
Lanois, Daniel 147
Led Zeppelin 96, 182, 202, 215, 218

Lennon, John 37, 61
Levin, Teri 171, 180
Levin, Tony 119, 156, 162, 168, 171, 180, 202,
Lindisfarne 100-101, 106
Little Feat 182
Livingstone, Bunny 190
Livingstone, Ken 157, 210-214
Lumley, Robin 178-183

Machat, Marty 196-197
Macphail, David (father) 16-19, 20, 26, 27, 41, 49, 62, 65, 218
Macphail, Doris Barbara (aunt) 16
Macphail, Kate (sister) 17-18, 25, 49, 55, 219
Macphail, Mary (née Ward) (mother) 16-20, 25, 29, 40, 41, 47, 61, 68, 77, 218
Macphail, Moira (sister) 17, 18, 49, 62, 219
Madonna 217
Maelen, Jimmy 156
Mahavishnu Orchestra 92, 178, 181
Mamoni, Willie 191
Marley, Bob 190
Marotta, Jerry 162-164, 168, 171, 179
Marotta, Rick 162
Maruga 162
Maw, Ray 210
Maxwell, Suzanne 136-139
May, Brian 96
Mayall, John, & Bluesbreakers, The 41-42, 96, 103
Mayall, Rod 103
Mayhew, John 68, 69, 70, 78, 81, 82
MC² (group) 201-203
McCartney, Paul 160, 212
McGinnis, Cindy 171, 173
McGinnis, Sid 162, 168, 171, 173
Meador, Steve 197
Mercury, Freddie 96
Merson, Vivienne 46-47
Meyer, Jack 43, 44
Moore, Sally 38, 164, 165

Moroccan Roll (Brand X) 178
Morrison, Van 193-196
Mott the Hoople 73
Muirhead, Denis 87-88
Munro, Murray 201-202
Munro, Sarah 201
Munt, Fred 51, 80, 91, 97, 122
Murray-Smith, Brian 182
'Musical Box, The' 103, 104, 109-110, 126, 128
Musical Box, The (Genesis tribute band) 148

N'Dour, Youssou 214
Newman, Dale 184-190
Nice, The 80
Nursery Cryme 102-103, 105, 107, 109, 226

O'Connor, Sinead 217
Oldham, Andrew Loog 35-36
'One Eyed Hound' 58
Ostermayer, Paul 197
Owen, Alan 136, 152

Page, Jimmy 194
Paine, Stephen 218
Pallenberg, Anita 43
Palmgren, Selim 110
'Pennsylvania Flickhouse' 36, 39, 50
Pert, Morris 178, 179, 183
Peter Gabriel ('Car' album) 156-157, 159, 160, 167, 168
Peter Gabriel ('Melt' album) 160, 167, 178, 214
Peter Gabriel ('Scratches' album) 160, 162, 166, 167
Phillips, Anthony 'Ant' 25, 55, 62, 64, 73, 73, 74, 75, 148, 213, 217; and Anon 34-35, 39; at Charterhouse 27-30, 53; at Christmas Cottage 69-72; formation of Genesis 53; leaves Genesis 81-82; recording first LP 54-55; stage fright 81
Pink Floyd 106, 166, 218, 223
Pitt, Kenneth 72

INDEX

Porcaro, Steve 216
Procol Harum 70
Purdie, Bernard 92

Queen 96

Rare Bird 74, 80
Reed, Michael 61, 112
Rebennack, Mac (aka Dr John) 195
Redding, Otis 39
'Return Of the Giant Hogweed, The' 147
Richard, Cliff 36
Richards, Keith 35, 41, 43, 78
Roberts, Brian 53
Robinson, Sharon 197-198
Rolling Stones, The 9, 25, 29, 30, 35, 36, 43, 46, 62, 107, 182
Rutherford, Angie 145
Rutherford, Mike 62, 64, 66, 73, 74, 75, 79, 82, 83, 85, 90, 95-97, 122, 128, 130, 133, 141, 143, 147, 148, 212, 213-214, 217; and Anon 34-35; as guitarist 108; at Charterhouse 33-34; at Christmas Cottage 69-73; autobiography (*The Living Years*) 33; formation of Genesis 53; recording first LP 54-55
Salvatore, Maurizio 112-113
Sams, Craig & Greg 101
Savoy Brown Blues Band, The 41-42
Scarlet and the Black, The 26
Schleyer, Hanns Martin 171
Schwartzberg, Alan 156
Selby, Adrian 114, 132
Selby, Gerard 76, 92, 94, 97, 112, 114
Selling England By the Pound 128, 134
Seraphino, Danny 180
'Silent Sun, The' 54
Silva, Jose 149
Silver, John 68
Bifferty, Skip 37
Sleep, Tony 206
'Slipper Man, The' 127

Small Faces, The 39
Smith, Graham 184-189
Smith, Tony 118, 132, 136, 146, 152, 153, 155, 160, 161, 177, 194, 215
'Solsbury Hill' 153, 155, 156
Spirit 202
Springsteen, Bruce 214
'Stagnation' 66, 71
Stansfield, Graham 74
Stanshall, Vivian 80
Status Quo 125
Steele, Tommy 25
Steely Dan 137
Steurmer, Daryl 214, 216
Stevens, Cat 93, 96, 143
Stewart, Chris 37, 55, 68
Stewart, Dave 151, 192
Stewart, Rod 37
Sting 214
Stopps, Dave 73
Stratton-Smith, Tony ('Strat') 51, 74, 75, 77, 78, 84, 87, 97, 100-103, 106, 108, 121, 122, 129, 146, 194, 196
String Driven Thing 184
Supertramp 181
'Supper's Ready' 109, 110, 126, 150, 152

Taylor, Elizabeth 42
Taylor, Roger 96
Thompson, Chester 127, 214
Thorgerson, Storm 166
Tosh, Peter 190-191
Toto 216
Townshend, Pete 104
Traffic 68, 195
Travers, Bill 25
Trespass 66, 71, 76, 80-82, 85, 92, 99
Trick Of the Tail 149, 151, 152
Troeller, Gordian 190
Turner, Ike & Tina 180
Tyrell, Marcia 33
Tyrell, Rob 28, 33

Uriah Heep 191

Van Der Graaf Generator 80, 101,
106, 183
Vaughan-Thomas, David 75
Wailers, The 190
'Waiting For the Big One' 168
Warnes, Jennifer 197-198
'Watcher Of the Skies' 94, 126, 128
Watkins, Mitch 197
Welch, Chris 54, 101, 128
Wentzell, Barrie 128
Western, Jimmy 76-77
White, Allan 126
Whitehead, Paul 126
Who, The 9, 128
Wilde, Marty 23, 25
Wilding, Michael 44
Williamson, Harry 47
'Willow Farm' 109
Wilson, Brian 125
Wonder, Stevie 37, 218
Wood, Chris 195
Wood, Ronnie 37

Yardbirds, The 9, 39, 63
Yes 92, 103, 106, 136, 151, 192
Yorke, Ritchie 194
Young, Neil 93

Zappa, Frank 128